Charles Nordhoff

California for Health, Pleasure, and Residence

A Book for Travellers and Settlers

Charles Nordhoff

California for Health, Pleasure, and Residence
A Book for Travellers and Settlers

ISBN/EAN: 9783337206253

Printed in Europe, USA, Canada, Australia, Japan

Cover: Foto ©Andreas Hilbeck / pixelio.de

More available books at **www.hansebooks.com**

FOR

HEALTH, PLEASURE, AND RESIDENCE

A BOOK FOR TRAVELLERS AND SETTLERS

NEW EDITION, THOROUGHLY REVISED

GIVING

DETAILED ACCOUNTS OF THE CULTURE OF THE WINE AND RAISIN GRAPE
THE ORANGE, LEMON, OLIVE, AND OTHER SEMI-TROPICAL FRUITS
COLONY SETTLEMENTS, METHODS OF IRRIGATION, ETC.

BY

CHARLES NORDHOFF

WITH MAPS AND NUMEROUS ILLUSTRATIONS

Entered according to Act of Congress, in the year 1882, by

HARPER & BROTHERS,

In the Office of the Librarian of Congress, at Washington.

All rights reserved.

PREFACE.

THERE have been Americans who saw Rome before they saw Niagara; and for one who has visited the Yosemite, a hundred will tell you about the Alps, and a thousand about Paris. Now, I have no objection to Europe; but I would like to induce Americans, when they contemplate a journey for health, pleasure, or instruction, or all three, to think also of their own country, and particularly of California, which has so many delights in store for the tourist, and so many attractions for the farmer or settler looking for a mild and healthful climate and a productive country.

When a Northern American visits a tropical country, be it Cuba, Mexico, Brazil, or Central America, he is delighted with the bright skies, the mild climate, the wonderful productiveness of the soil, and the novel customs of the inhabitants; but he is repelled by an enervating atmosphere, by the dread of malarious diseases, by the semi-barbarous habits of the people, and often by a lawless state of society. Moreover, he must leave his own country, and is without the comfort and security he enjoys at home. California is our own; and it is the first tropical land which our race has thoroughly mastered and made itself at home in. There, and there only, on this planet, the traveller and resident may enjoy the delights of the tropics without their penalties; a mild climate, not enervating, but healthful and health-restoring; a wonderfully and variously productive soil, without tropical malaria; the grandest scenery, with perfect security and comfort in travelling arrangements; strange customs, but neither lawlessness nor semi-barbarism.

The first part of this book will interest mainly travellers and tourists, and in it I have aimed to give a plain and detailed statement of the routes across the continent, and of what the traveller should see by the way; of the notable sights of California, and how they may best be visited; and a table of expenses, and of the time needed for different excursions. There is also a chapter on health resorts for invalids. Consumptives, and persons debilitated by age, overwork, or disease, will find in some localities in Southern California a climate remarkably mild and healing.

In this revised edition of my work on California I have had to note so many new matters that the book is almost entirely re-written. The first edition was published nine years ago. In that time very great changes have come about in California—changes which make the State far more interesting to the traveller and sight-seer, more comfortable to the seeker for health, and more valuable and important to the settler, than it was when I first wrote.

The tourist and sight-seer has now the advantage of a number of new railroads, enabling him to penetrate rapidly, and with ease and comfort, parts of the State which when this book first appeared were accessible only by stage or horseback journey.

The seeker after health has open to him a larger choice of pleasant health-resorts, and, what is of greater importance, he will now find, what then was unattainable, well-arranged, well-appointed, and thoroughly comfortable hotels and inns, where even the most delicate invalids may rest with enjoyment. To the health-seeker this is a matter of the first importance; and well-cooked and well-served food, sunny rooms, open fires, broad piazzas sheltered from the wind by glass enclosures—all these now supplement the natural advantages of such places as Santa Barbara, San Gabriel, and the Ojai.

To the agriculturist looking for a new home the changes and developments in the agricultural parts of California during the last nine years have substantially opened a new and vast field of varied products; and to these I have given a number of chapters.

The new cultures and new methods which have been introduced since I first wrote of its agricultural capabilities have produced great and often startling effects. All that I foretold in the first edition of this book has been realized, and more too. Great tracts which had the appearance of sterile desert when I saw them in 1872 are now literally "blossoming as the rose." The extension of irrigation has not merely enabled farmers to plant and sow where nine years ago sheep got but a scanty living, but in the mild climate of California trees and shrubs have grown so rapidly that, to my amazement, I found many places which on my last visit were bare and apparently sterile plains, now presenting already the appearance of old-settled farming tracts—trees forty and fifty feet high shading the roads; apples, standard pears, grapes, and a great variety of other fruits, in bearing, and a multitude of pleasant and prosperous homes and farmsteads where nine, and even eight, years ago I drove or rode fifty or a hundred miles without seeing a tree or a house.

An intelligent traveller in California ought to give himself time to see something more than the great sights of the State. An English gentleman told me that the Yosemite itself was worth the long journey from England, and he was right; but to see somewhat of the wine, raisin, wheat, orange, and general orchard culture of the State is in itself a great novelty and pleasure, all the methods of the farmers are so different, often so ingenious, and the results are so surprising. The Californian farms with brains; in the pursuit of agriculture he has had constantly to devise new methods; and he has become a surprisingly intelligent man, because he has been engaged in a contest with nature in which ingenuity and fertility of resource have enabled him to conquer.

To the intending settler I will say that the broader experience gained by the farmers and orchardists of California in the last ten years gives new-comers very great advantages. It is now pretty well known what are the best ways to manage land, and what it can best and most profitably produce. New tools, new plants, new varieties, new methods, have been invented and brought in, and the farmer now settling himself in California has the advantage of all this experience gained.

To farmers, or wine and raisin growers, proposing to settle in California I recommend the reading of the chapter on "Colonies." A sufficiently large experience now proves that this method of settlement offers peculiar chances for success in the State; and it is my belief, founded on what I have seen, that a number of families settling together on a tract of land secure very many advantages which the isolated farmer is deprived of, and increase considerably their prospects, not only of satisfactory results but of comfort and happiness in the earlier period of their experiment.

CONTENTS.

CHAPTER I.
The Way Out, and Sight-seeing in California 17

CHAPTER II.
The Central Pacific Railroad 31

CHAPTER III.
The Tourist in California.—What to See, and How to See it 45

CHAPTER IV.
The Farallon Islands 63

CHAPTER V.
Southern California for Invalids 77

CHAPTER VI.
The Agricultural Wealth of California.—The Great Valleys 93

CHAPTER VII.
The Agricultural Lands and Peculiarities of California 100

CHAPTER VIII.
Grapes and Wine 113

CHAPTER IX.
Raisin-making 119

CHAPTER X.
Semi-tropical Fruits 125

CHAPTER XI.
Canning and Drying Fruits 132

CHAPTER XII.
Alfalfa 135

CONTENTS.

CHAPTER XIII.
Irrigation 140

CHAPTER XIV.
Settlement in Colonies 147

CHAPTER XV.
Hints to Small Farmers and Laborers 161

CHAPTER XVI.
A Night Around a Camp-fire 173

CHAPTER XVII.
A California Cattle Rancho.—A Rodeo.—Peculiar Customs of the Spanish Californians 185

APPENDIX.

Southern California for Consumptives 199
Tables of Temperature at San Bernardino, California 202
Tables of Temperature at Santa Barbara, California 205
Highest, Lowest, and Average Temperature at Santa Barbara, for each Month and Year from January 1, 1871, to January 1, 1882 206
Number of Days during which the Temperature fell below 43° or rose above 83° 206
Table of Comparative Temperatures 206
Monthly Mean Humidity, Saturation being 100° 206
Monthly Mean Temperature of Sea-water 206

ILLUSTRATIONS.

	PAGE
Map of the Pacific Coast, showing Points of Special Interest to Tourists	*Frontispiece.*
View from the Cliff House, San Francisco	17
Green Bluffs	22
Piute Squaw and Papoose	26
"The Loop"	29
Indian Sweat-house	31
Snow-sheds on the Central Pacific Railroad	34
Interior of Snow-shed, Central Pacific Railroad	35
First Office of the Central Pacific Railroad	38
Alkali Desert, Central Pacific Railroad	41
C. P. Huntington	43
Rounding Cape Horn	45
The Sentinel, Yosemite Valley	47
Eagle Gap, on the Truckee River	50
The Three Brothers, Yosemite Valley	53
The Geysers	55
Yosemite Falls	56
South Dome, Yosemite Valley	57
Plan of the Yosemite Valley	59
Nevada Fall, Yosemite Valley	61
Cathedral Rocks, Yosemite Valley	62
Running the Rookeries — Gathering Murre Eggs	63
Light-house of the South Farallon	66
Sea-lions	68
Shags, Murres, and Sea-gulls	70
The Gull's Nest	71
Arch at West End, Farallon Islands	72
A Contest for the Eggs	74
The Great Rookery	75

	PAGE
Snow-plough on the Central Pacific Railroad	77
Summit of the Sierras, from Central Pacific Railroad	79
Bloomer Cut, Central Pacific Railroad	81
A Bird's-eye View of the Transcontinental Route	83
The Yosemite Valley	86
Map of the San Joaquin Valley, California	88
Map of the Sacramento Valley, California	90
El Capitan	93
The Big Trees	96
Flume and Railroad at Gold Run, Sixty-four Miles from Sacramento	97
View of the Yosemite from the Mariposa Trail	100
View near the State Line, Truckee River	103
Lake Tahoe	107
"Prospecting"	110
"Panning Out"	111
A California Vineyard	113
Wine Vats	114
Training the Vine	115
A Bottling-cellar	117
"Cradle-rocking"	119
Indian Rancheria	121
The Mexican Arastra	125
Coast View, Mendocino County	132
Wood-chopper at Work	135
Point Arena Light-house	137
Boating on Donner Lake	140

ILLUSTRATIONS.

	PAGE
Donner Lake, Crested Peak, and Mount Lincoln	143
California Live-oak	145
The Bridal-veil Fall	147
Mirror Lake, Yosemite Valley	151
North Dome, Yosemite Valley	157
View from the Coulterville Trail	161
Secret Town—Trestle from the East, 1100 Feet Long, 90 Feet High	164
Winnowing Gold near Chinese Camp	165
Vernal Fall, Yosemite Valley	167
Hydraulic Mining at French Corral	169
Observation Car	170
Northern California	171
A Quartz Mill	173
A Flume	175
A Water-jam of Logs, Mendocino County	177
Flutter-wheel, on the Tuolumne	179
Turning a River	181
Coast View, Northern California	185
Piedras Blancas Light-house	186
Saw-mill on the Mendocino Coast	189
Shipping Lumber, Mendocino County	192
Point Reyes	195
Central Pacific Railroad Hospital	196

VIEW FROM THE CLIFF HOUSE, SAN FRANCISCO.

CALIFORNIA:

FOR HEALTH, PLEASURE, AND RESIDENCE.

CHAPTER I.

THE WAY OUT, AND SIGHT-SEEING IN CALIFORNIA.

THOUGH California has been celebrated in books, newspapers, and magazines for more than twenty years, it is really but little better known to the tourist—a creature who ought to know it thoroughly, to his own delight—as it was to Swift when he wrote, in his description of the flying island of Laputa: "The continent of which this kingdom is a part extends itself, as I have reason to believe, eastward to that unknown tract of America westward of California, and north to the Pacific Ocean, which is not above a hundred and fifty miles from Logado," and so on.

California is to most Eastern people still a land of big beets and pumpkins, of rough miners, of pistols, bowie-knives, abundant fruit, queer wines, high prices—full of discomforts, and abounding in dangers to the peaceful traveller. A New Yorker, inefficient except in his own business, looking to the government, municipal, State, or Federal, for almost everything except his daily dollars; overridden by a semi-barbarous foreign population; troubled with incapable servants, private as well as public; subject to daily rudeness from car-drivers and others who ought to be civil; rolled helplessly and tediously down-town to his business in a lumbering omnibus; exposed to inconveniences, to dirty streets, bad gas, beggars, loss of time through improper conveyances; to high taxes, theft, and all kinds of public wrong, year in and year out—this New Yorker fondly imagines himself to be living at the centre of civilization, and pities the unlucky friend who is "going to California." He invites him to dine before he sets out, "because you will not get a good dinner again till you return, you know;" he sends him, with his parting blessing, a heavy navy revolver; and shudders at the annoyances and dangers which his friend, out of a rash and venturesome disposition, is about to undergo.

Well, the New Yorker is mistaken. There are no dangers to travellers on the beaten track in California; there are no inconveniences which a child or a tenderly reared woman would not laugh at; they dine in San Francisco rather better, and with quite as much form and a more elegant and perfect service, than in New York; the San Francisco hotels are the best and cheapest in the world; the noble art of cooking is better understood in California than anywhere else in America where I have eaten; the bread is far better, the variety of food is greater; the persons with whom a tourist comes in contact, and upon whom his comfort and pleasures so greatly depend, are more uniformly civil, obliging, honest, and intelligent than they are anywhere in this country, or, so far as I know, in Europe; the pleasure-roads in the neighborhood of San Francisco are unequalled anywhere; the common country roads are kept in far better order than anywhere in the Eastern States; and when you have spent half a dozen weeks in the State, you will perhaps return with a notion that New York is the true frontier land, and that you have nowhere in the United States seen so comfortable a civilization—in all material points, that is to say—as you found in California.

If this seems incredible to what out there they call an Eastern person, let him reflect for a moment upon the fact that New York receives a constant supply of the rudest, least civilized European populations; that of the immigrants landed at Castle Garden, the neediest, the least thrifty and energetic, and the most vicious remain in New York, while the ablest and most valuable fly rapidly westward; and that, besides this, New York has necessarily a large population of native adventurers; while, on the other hand, California has a settled and permanent population of doubly picked men.

"When the gold was discovered," said a Californian to whom I had expressed my wonder at the admirable *quality* of much of the State's population, "wherever an Eastern family had three or four boys, the ablest, the most energetic one, came hither. Of that great multitude of picked men, again, the weakly broke down under the strain; they died of disease or bad whiskey, or they returned home. The remainder you see here, and you ought not to wonder that they are above your Eastern average in intelligence, energy, and thrift. Moreover, you are to remember that, contrary to the commonly received belief, California has a more settled population than almost any State in the Union. It does not change; our people cannot 'move West,' and very few of them return to the East. What we have we keep, and almost all, except the Chinese, have a permanent interest in the State. Finally," added this old miner, who is now a banker, and whom you could not tell from a New Yorker, either in his dress or the tones of his voice, or in the manner in which he transacts business, and who yet has not been "home," as he calls it, for many years—"finally, you must remember that of our immigrants who came from China, not a single one, so far as is known, but knew how to read, write, and keep at least his own accounts on his own abacus when he passed the Golden Gate. We are not saints out here, but I believe we have much less of a frontier population than you in New York." And my experience persuades me that he was right.

Certainly in no part of the continent is pleasure-travelling so exquisite and unalloyed a pleasure as in California. Not only are the sights grand, wonderful, and surprising in the highest degree, but the climate is exhilarating and favorable to an active life; the weather is so certain that you need not lose a day, and may lay out your whole tour in the State without reference to rainy days, unless it is in the rainy season: the roads are surprisingly good, the country inns are clean, the beds good, the food abundant and almost always well cooked, and the charges moderate: and the journey by rail from New York to San Francisco, which costs little more than the steamer fare to London, and is shorter than a voyage across the Atlantic, is in itself delightful as well as instructive. Probably twenty Americans go to Europe for one who goes to California; for one who has seen the Yosemite, a hundred will tell you of the Alps, and a thousand about Paris; yet no American who has not seen the Plains, the Great Salt Lake, the Sierra Nevada, and the wonders of California, can honestly say that he has seen his own country, or that he even has an intelligent idea of its greatness. It is of this journey from New York to San Francisco that I wish to give in this chapter some details which will, I hope, tempt many who contemplate a European tour to turn their faces westward rather, sure that this way lies the most real pleasure.

California is attainable now by either of two routes, one by the Union and Central Pacific roads, beginning at Omaha; the other by way of the Atchison, Topeka, and Santa Fé from Kansas City, or by way of New Orleans, both these lines connecting with the Southern Pacific Railroad. It is best to go out one way and return by the other; on all the roads comfortable parlor and sleeping cars make the journey pleasant, the changes are infrequent, and every care is taken to make the traveller comfortable. The travelling time from New York to San Francisco, by Omaha or Kansas City, is seven days. If you go out by the Union Pacific, you should stop a day or two at Salt Lake City. If by the Kansas City route, you should not omit a day or two at Santa Fé.

At Chicago or St. Louis the journey to California really begins. In the East we make journeys by rail; west of Chicago men live on the cars. In the East a railroad journey is an interruption to our lives. We submit to it, because no one has yet been ingenious enough to contrive a flying-machine, and the telegraph wires do not carry passengers by lightning; but we submit to it reluctantly; we travel by night in order to escape the tedium of the journey, and no one thinks of amusing himself on the cars. When you leave Omaha or Kansas City you take up your residence on the train. The cars are no longer a ferry to carry you across a short distance; you are to live in them for days and nights; and no Eastern man knows the comfort or pleasure of travelling by rail until he crosses the Plains.

I suspect that part of our discomfort in making a railroad journey comes from its brevity. You are unsettled; the car, on a common journey, is but a longer ferry; and who ever thought of taking his ease on a ferry-boat? You cannot fix your mind on the present; your constant thought is of when you will get there. Now the journey to San Francisco takes not a few hours, but a number of days; and when you are safely embarked on the train at Chicago or St. Louis, you leave care behind in the depot, and make yourself comfortable, as one does on a sea-voyage.

Moreover, until you have taken this journey, you will never know how great a difference it makes to your comfort whether your train goes at the rate of forty or at twenty-two miles per hour. This last is the pace of the iron horse between Omaha or Kansas City and San Francisco; and it is to the fierce and rapid rush of an Eastern lightning express what a gentle and easy amble is to a rough and jolting trot. It would not be surprising to find that the overland journey will, by-and-by, create a public opinion in favor of what New Yorkers would call slow trains. Certainly a lightning express rushing through from Chicago to San Francisco would not carry any one, except an express-man, a second time. At forty or forty-five miles per hour the country you pass through is a blur; one hardly sees between the telegraph poles; pleasure and ease are alike out of question; reading tires your eyes, writing is impossible, conversation impracticable except at the auctioneer pitch, and the motion is wearing and tiresome. But at twenty-two miles per hour travel by rail is a different affair; and having unpacked your books and unstrapped your wraps in your Pullman or Central Pacific palace-car, you may pursue all sedentary avocations and amusements of a parlor at home; and as your house-keeping is done—and admirably done—for you by alert and experienced servants; as you may lie down at full length or sit up, sleep or wake, at your choice; as your dinner is sure to be abundant, very tolerably cooked, and not hurried; as you are pretty certain to make acquaintances on the car; and as the country through which you pass is strange, and abounds in curious and interesting sights, and the air is fresh and exhilarating—you soon fall into the ways of the voyage; and if you are a tired business man, or a wearied house-keeper, your careless ease will be such a rest as certainly most busy and overworked Americans know how to enjoy.

You write very comfortably at a table in your section; books and photographs lie on the table; your wife sits at the window, sewing and looking out on long ranges of snow-clad mountains, or on boundless, ocean-like plains; children play on the floor, or watch at the windows for the comical prairie-dogs sitting near their holes and turning laughable somersaults as the car sweeps by. You converse as you would in your parlor at home; the noise of the train is as much lost to your consciousness as the steamship's rush through the waters; the air is pure, for these cars are thoroughly ventilated; the heating apparatus used seems to me

GREEN BLUFFS.

quite perfect, for it keeps the feet warm, and diffuses an agreeable and equal heat through all parts of the car.

As at sea, so here, the most important events of the day are your meals. The porter calls you at any hour you appoint in the morning; he gives you half an hour's notice of breakfast, dinner, or supper; and the conductor tells you not to hurry, but to eat at your ease, for he will not leave any one behind. Your beds are made up and your room or section swept and aired while you are at breakfast, or before if you are early risers; you find both water and fresh towels abundant; ice is put into the tank which supplies drinking-water, at the most improbable places in the great wilderness; and an attentive servant is always within call, and comes to you at intervals during the day to ask if you need anything to make you more contented.

About eight o'clock—for, as at sea, you keep good hours—the porter, in a clean gray uniform like that of a Central Park policeman, comes in to make up the beds. The freshest and whitest of linen and brightly colored blankets complete the outfit; and you undress and go to bed as you would at home, and, unless you have eaten too heartily of antelope or elk, will sleep as soundly.

Thus you ride onward, day after day, toward the setting sun, and unless you are an extremely unhappy traveller, your days will be filled with pleasure from the novel sights by the way.

Between Chicago or St. Louis and the crossing of the Missouri River your train will carry a dining-car, which is a great curiosity in its way. I expected to find this somewhat greasy, a little untidy, and with a smell of the kitchen. It might, we travellers thought, be a convenience, but it could hardly be a luxury. But in fact it is as neat, as nicely fitted, as trim and cleanly, as though Delmonico had furnished it; and though the kitchen may be in the forward end of the car, so perfect is the ventilation that there is not even the faintest odor of cooking. You sit at little tables which comfortably accommodate four persons; you order your breakfast, dinner, or supper from a bill of fare which contains a quite surprising number of dishes, and you eat, from snow-white linen and neat dishes, admirably cooked food, and pay a moderate price.

Beyond the Missouri River you eat at stations placed at proper distances apart, where abundant provision is made, and the food is, for the most part, both well cooked and well served. These hotel stations are under the supervision and control of the managers of the roads. Sufficient time is allowed — from twenty-five to thirty minutes — to eat; the conductor tells you beforehand that a bell will be rung five minutes before the train starts, and we always found him obliging enough to look in and tell the ladies to take their time, as he would not leave them behind.

There is a pleasant spice of variety and adventure in getting out by the way-side at the eating stations. We saw strange faces, we had time to look about us, the occasional Indian delighted the children, we stretched our legs, and saw something of our fellow-passengers in the other cars. Moreover, if you have a numerous party desirous to eat together, the porter will telegraph ahead for you to have a sufficient number of seats reserved, and thus you take your places without flurry or haste, and do not have your digestion spoiled by preliminary and vexatious thoughts about pushing for a good place. In short, these trains are managed for the pleasure and accommodation of the passengers. The journey would, I suppose, be unendurable else.

On the whole, a company of three or four can travel the most enjoyably across the continent; and there is no reason why a man should not take his children, if they are ten years old or over, as well as his wife. Four fill a drawing-room, three or four can be comfortable in a section on a sleeping-car; and in California, if you have three or four in your party, you can travel as cheaply by private carriage as by stage to the few notable sights of the State which you do not reach by rail, and thus add much to the comfort and pleasure of such journeys. And from the hour you leave the Missouri River you will find everything new, curious, and wonderful; the plains, with their buffalo, antelope, and prairie-dogs; the mountains, which lift up their glorious snow-clad summits; the deep cañons and gorges through which your train finds its way westward; the stretch of desert, the alkali and sage-brush, all are novel and interesting; and as you journey onward day after day, and night after night, you begin for the first time to comprehend how vast is our country, how great its resources; and as you see how slowly but surely agriculture pushes into what used to be called the "Great American Desert," you perceive that there is still abundant room for the millions who are rushing over to us from Europe.

On the plains and in the mountains the railroad will seem to you the great fact. Man seems but an accessary; he appears to exist only that the road may be worked; and I never appreciated until I crossed the Plains the grand character of the old Romans as road-builders, or the real importance of good roads. We, too, in this generation are road-builders. Neither the desert nor the sierra stops us; there is no such word as "impossible" to men like Huntington—they build railroads in the full faith that population and wealth will follow on their iron track.

And they seem to be the best explorers. The "Great American Desert," which we school-boys thirty or forty years ago saw on the map of North America, has disappeared at the snort of the iron horse: coal and iron are found to abound on the plains as soon as the railroad kings have need of them; the very desert becomes fruitful; and at Humboldt Wells, on the Central Pacific Railroad, in the midst of the sage-brush and alkali country, you will see corn, wheat, potatoes, and fruits of different kinds growing luxuriantly, with the help of culture and irrigation; proving that this vast tract, long supposed to be worthless, needs only skilful treatment to become valuable.

One cannot help but speculate upon what kind of men we Americans shall be when all these now desolate plains are filled; when cities shall be found where now only the lonely depot or the infrequent cabin stands; when the iron and coal of these regions shall have become, as they soon must, the foundation of great manufacturing populations; and when, perhaps, the whole continent will be covered by our Stars and Stripes. No other nation has ever spread over so large a territory or so diversified a surface as ours. From the low, sea-washed shores of the Atlantic your California journey carries you over boundless plains which lie nearly as high as the summit of Mount Washington. Americans are digging silver ore in Colorado, three thousand feet higher than the highest point of the White Mountains. At Virginia City, in Nevada, one of the busiest centres of mining, the traveller finds it hard to draw in breath enough for rapid motion; and many persons, when they first arrive there, suffer from bleeding at the nose by reason of the rarity of the air. Again, in Maine half the farmer's year is spent in accumulating supplies for the other and frozen half; all over the Northern States the preparation for winter is an important part of our lives; but in San Francisco the winter is the pleasantest part of the year; in Los Angeles they do not think it needful to build fireplaces, and scarcely chimneys, in their houses. And one people, speaking the same language, reading the same books, holding a common religion, paying taxes to the same government, and proud of one common flag, pervades these various altitudes and climates, intervisits, intercommunicates, intermarries, and is, with the potent help of the railroad, fused constantly more closely together as a nation. What manner of man, think you, will be the American of 1982, the product of so many different climes, of so various a range as to altitude?

I wrote that on the plains and on the mountains the railroad is the one great fact. Whatever you notice by the way that is the handiwork of man, appears to be there mainly for your convenience or safety who are passing over the road. On the Union Pacific you see miles upon miles of snow-fences. On the Central Pacific, thirty or forty miles of solid snow-sheds, thoroughly built, and fully guarded by gangs of laborers, make the passage safe in the severest snow-storms. Great snow-ploughs, eleven feet high, stand at intervals on the plains and in the mountains, ready to drive, with three or four, or even seven or eight, locomotives behind them, the snow out of the cuts. The telegraph accompanies you on your whole long journey. Coal-mines are opened to furnish fuel to your locomotive. At intervals of a hundred miles, night and day, you hear men beating the wheels of a train to see if they are sound. Everywhere you find yourself cared for by a multitude of men whose main reason for existence seems to be this care.

If you go out by the Southern route, you may stop off at Las Vegas, and drive over to the Hot Springs near there, where excellent hotel accommodations and a warm bath will rest and refresh you. But you should not omit on any account to leave your train at Lamy, and take a branch line of eighteen miles to Santa Fé, where you should spend a day or two. It is a quaint and notable old Mexican town, full of curiosities for the traveller.

Passing over the Union Pacific road, you should give a day to Salt Lake City. It lies two hours and a half by rail from Ogden, where the Union and Central Pacific lines meet. Salt Lake need not hold any mere pleasure traveller more than a day. You can drive all over it in two hours; and when you have seen the Tabernacle—an admirably-arranged and very ugly building—which contains an organ, built in Salt Lake by an English workman, a Mormon named Ridges, which organ is second in size only to the Boston organ; the Menagerie, which contains several bears, some lynxes and wild-cats—natives of these mountains—and a small but interesting collection of minerals and Indian remains, and of the manufactures of the Mormons; the Temple Block; and enjoyed the magnificent view which is seen from the back of the city of the valley, the

PIUTE SQUAW AND PAPOOSE.

Great Lake, and the snow-capped peaks which lie on the other side—a view which you carry with you all over the place—you have done Salt Lake City, and have time, if you have risen early, to bathe at the sulphur spring. The lake lies too far away to be visited in one day.

Of Mormonism you will see all that is left: it is a decaying system; and the dread and silence with which traveller or trader was forced to move about Salt Lake City fifteen years ago has so utterly disappeared, that you may now openly buy photographs of Mormon "families," where the man sits in front of his cabin, with his numerous wives engaged in their weary labors around him, looking like what they really are, his bondwomen, who serve him in the place of the hired help whom he could not afford to hire. Railroads, mines, and contact with the world have broken the back of the Mormon tyranny.

In planning your journey you will desire to know how much time is required, and what the expense of your trip will be. Here are three schedules or time-tables for tours of various lengths, and a general estimate of expenses:

FOR A FIVE WEEKS' TOUR.

	Days.
From Chicago or St. Louis to San Francisco	5
At Salt Lake or Santa Fé	1
San Francisco	4
San José, Monterey, Santa Cruz	4
The Geysers	3
The Yosemite, stopping 2 days in the valley and 1 day at the Big Trees	1
Los Angeles	8
Santa Fé or Salt Lake	2
Return journey	5
	33

Leaving one day to spare.

If you have another week, you can add to the above a visit to Lake Tahoe, Donner Lake, and Virginia City. With seven weeks, you will have time to go also, in addition to the above, to Mount Shasta, for which you set out from Sacramento; and this journey will show you the great Sacramento valley.

It must not be forgotten that on his way to these special sights the traveller passes through many interesting places. For instance, on his way to the Geysers he will see the beautiful Napa valley; Calistoga, with its hot springs and petrified forest; and San Rafael, one of the most charming nooks in the State. The Mariposa grove of Big Trees he sees on his way from Madera to the Yosemite. The fertile San Joaquin valley, a region as rich as the Nile, he passes through between Madera and Los Angeles. Near Los Angeles, and connected by railroad, lies the very successful colony of Anaheim, and near San Bernardino lies the equally successful Riverside colony. A day or two spent at Marysville will enable the tourist to see something of the mining region of California, placer and quartz, as well as the famous Yuba dam. Near San José, and within an afternoon's drive, are the Almaden quicksilver mines.

The best time to see California is in the spring of the year, when everything is green, and the whole State is enchanting. The visitor who can set out in the latter part of March will do well to take the Southern route, returning by way of the Central and Union Pacific. The following is a statement of necessary expenses for such a journey as I have sketched:

Fare by railroad from Chicago, by Omaha and Ogden, to San Francisco...	$115
Return, by Southern Pacific and Atchison, Topeka, and Santa Fé railroads, to St. Louis	112
To Salt Lake and return	5
Truckee to Lake Tahoe and return (stage)	4
Geysers, going by Calistoga and back by Cloverdale	16
Madera to Yosemite and back	40
Monterey and Santa Cruz and return	5—297
Add berth on sleeping-car:	
Chicago to San Francisco by Omaha and Ogden	$17
San Francisco to St. Louis by Deming and Kansas City	16
	33
Meals, two per day = $2 a day, for ten days	20— 53
	$350

The remaining expenses during a tour of five weeks, such as hotel bills, horses and guides in the Yosemite valley, carriages elsewhere, etc., will be amply covered by $125; and if you allow five hundred dollars for the excursion of five weeks, sketched above, you will have enough to buy some curiosities to carry home with you, and will have stopped at first-class hotels everywhere, and used a carriage wherever it was convenient.

Los Angeles and San Bernardino you see on the Southern route without extra expense. Santa Barbara and San Diego are reached only by stage or carriage from points on the Southern Pacific road. If you have time and inclination to see Mount Shasta, this will cost you $30 for the railroad and stage fares from Sacramento and return, and about five dollars a day for the time you give to it.

I append here, as matter interesting to the tourist, the elevation above and depression below sea-level of some principal points on both routes.

At Omaha, crossing the Missouri River on the Union Pacific Railroad, your elevation above sea-level is 966 feet.

At Cheyenne you are 6041 feet above the sea, and only 387 feet below the top of Mount Washington.

Sherman, 8242 feet, is the highest point on the journey. Laramie is 7136 feet above the sea; Ogden, 4301; and from this point—still higher than most of the White Mountain peaks—you rise again on the line of the Central Pacific, the elevation of principal points, going west of Ogden, being: Elko, 5063 feet; Winnemucca, 4332; Reno, 4497; Truckee, 5819; Summit, the highest point on the Central Pacific, 7017; from which point the train runs down in three hours to Colfax, only 2422 feet elevation, and in less than four hours more to Sacramento, which stands but 30 feet above tide-water.

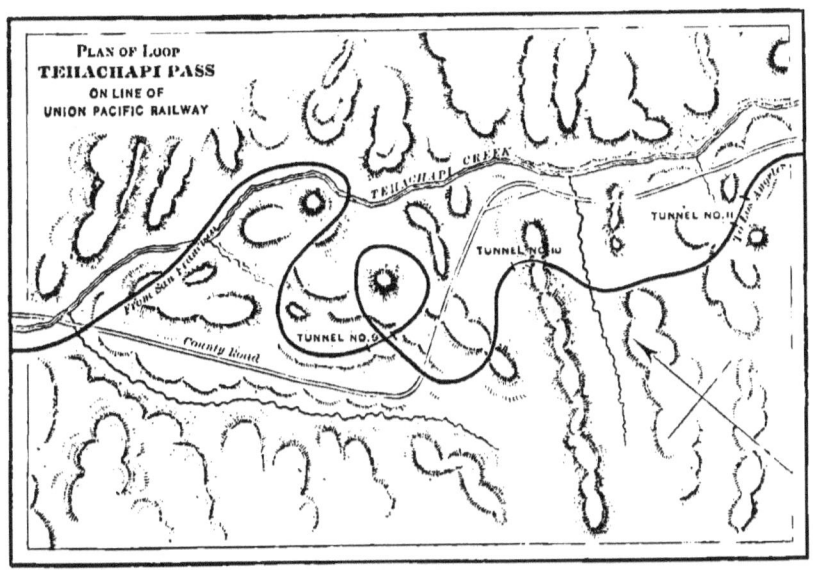

"THE LOOP."

Going eastward, over the Southern Pacific and Atchison, Topeka, and Santa Fé roads, your elevation above the sea is 26 feet at Lathrop, 278 feet at Madera, the station for the Yosemite valley; 3964 feet at Tehachapi Summit; 1401 at the San Fernando Tunnel; only 293 at Los Angeles; 2560 at San Gorgonio, from which height your train carries you down to Indio, 20 feet below the sea-level, Dos Palmas 253 feet below, and Frink's Spring 260 feet below the ocean. For sixty-one miles your train runs below sea-level. At Yuma you have risen again to 140 feet above tide; at Tucson you are 2390 feet above; at Deming, 4334 feet; at Albuquerque, 5006; at Lamy, the station for Santa Fé, 6531; at Glorietta, 7587; at Las Vegas, 6452; at Granada, 3468; at Topeka, 904; and at Kansas City, where once more you cross the Missouri River, 765 feet above the sea.

On the Southern Pacific Railroad, between Keene and Girard, 352 miles from San Francisco, you should notice a remarkable feat of engineering. In surmounting a natural obstacle, the railroad turns completely upon itself, and forms what they call a Loop, the line crossing itself. The length of this loop is 3795 feet; the elevations are: at the Tunnel No. 9, 2956; at the upper grade, over Tunnel No. 9, 3034 feet; the upper turn being 78 feet above the lower. The engraving on the preceding page represents the plan of this engineering curiosity.

The object of making this "loop" was to secure a proper and safe grade in descending from the mountains to the plain, the natural descent being too abrupt.

The San Fernando Tunnel is 6967 feet in length, being one of the longest railroad tunnels in America. It is between Newhall and San Fernando, on the Southern Pacific Railroad, 456 miles from San Francisco and 26 miles from Los Angeles.

INDIAN SWEAT-HOUSE.

CHAPTER II.

THE CENTRAL PACIFIC RAILROAD.

YOU may enter or leave California by one of the most notable objects it contains—I mean the Central Pacific Railroad. All the world has heard of the great Mont Cenis Tunnel; and travellers tell us perpetually of sights and public works in Europe; but, if the Americans were not the most modest people in the world, they would before this have made more famous than any European public work the magnificent and daring piece of engineering by whose help you roll speedily and luxuriously across the Sierra Nevada from Ogden to San Francisco. But we Americans have too much to do to spend our time in boasting. When we have accomplished some great thing, we turn to something still greater, if it is at hand; and it is a curious commentary upon this characteristic that the man whose daring, determination, resistless energy, and clear prevision did more than anything else to build this great road—I mean C. P. Huntington—has already turned away to other enterprises, in parts almost equally difficult.*

---

* There is a story of Huntington, which is so characteristic of him and of the spirit of Yankee boys, that I venture to relate it here. He was one of a large family, I have been told—children of a poor and hard-working Connecticut man. The children knew that they would have to fight their own way in the world, and young Huntington's first dollar was earned when he was less than twelve years of age. A well-to-do neighbor employed the boy to pile up in the wood-shed a quantity of firewood which had been sawed for the winter. He piled it neatly and smoothly, and this done, with that spirit of thoroughness with which, in middle age, he built railroads, he picked up all the chips in the wood-yard, and swept it clean with an old broom. His employer was much

You take the cars of the Central Pacific Railroad at Ogden, at a level of 4200 feet above the sea, and the locomotive draws your train over many miles of an alkali desert, in parts of which water had to be drawn forty miles for the men who built the road; up the Sierra to a height of 7017 feet, where the snow lay sixty feet deep one winter while the road was building, and where they actually dug tunnels through the snow and ice to work on the road-bed; down from the summit around cliffs, along the edge of precipices, through miles of snow-sheds, through tunnels and deep rock-cuts, across chasms where you shudder as you look down into the rushing torrent far below; and all this, until you reach the plain of the Sacramento, through a country believed at the time to be uninhabitable, and presenting at every step the most tremendous difficulties to the engineer as well as to the capitalist.

The story of the building of the Central Pacific Railroad is one of the most remarkable examples of the dauntless spirit of American enterprise. The men who built it were merchants, who probably knew no more about building railroads, when they had passed middle age and attained a respectable competence by trade, than a Colusa Pike knows about Greek. Huntington and Hopkins were hardware merchants. Stanford was at one time a wholesale dealer in groceries, though later Governor of the State; the two Crockers were dry-goods men. These five, all at or past middle age, all living in Sacramento, then an insignificant interior town of California, believing in each other, believing that the railroad must be built, and finding no one else ready to undertake it, put their hands and heads and their means to the great work, and carried it through.

Everybody knows what is the common fate in this country of railroad projectors. A few sanguine and public-spirited men procure a charter, make up a company, subscribe for the stock, drag all their friends in, get the preliminary surveys made, begin the work—and then break down; and two or three capitalists, who have been quietly waiting for this foreseen conclusion—foreseen by them, I mean—thereupon step in, buy the valuable wreck for a song, and build and run and own the road. This is a business in itself. Dozens of men have made millions apiece by this process, which is perfectly legitimate; for, as the French say, in order to

---

pleased with the boy's work, and, patting him on the head, gave him a dollar, and said, "You have done this so well, that I guess I'll have to give you the job next year again." "My mind was divided," said Huntington, later in life, when he related this incident, "between delight at the dollar and the praise, and contempt for the man who thought that I should be at no better work than piling wood in a year from then."

succeed you must be successful; or, as we say in this country, to the victors belong the spoils.

Now the projectors of the Central Pacific Railroad completed it, and to-day control and manage it; they did not let it slip out of their fingers; and, what is more, being only merchants, totally inexperienced in railroad building and railroad managing, they did their work so well that, in the opinion of the best engineers, their road is to-day one of the most thoroughly built and equipped and best-managed in the United States. Their bonds sell in Europe but little if any below United States Government bonds, and their credit as a company, in London, Frankfort, and Paris, is as high as that of the Government itself.

Moreover, you are to remember that these five Sacramento merchants, who undertook to build a railroad through eight hundred miles of an almost uninhabited country, over mountains and across an alkali desert, were totally unknown to the great money world; that their project was pronounced impracticable by engineers of reputation testifying before legislative committees; that it was opposed and ridiculed at every step by the moneyed men of San Francisco; that even in their own neighborhood they were thought sure to fail; and the "Dutch Flat Swindle," as their project was called, was caricatured, written down in pamphlets, abused in newspapers, spoken against by politicians, denounced by capitalists, and for a long time held in such ill-repute that it was more than a banker's character for prudence was worth to connect himself with it, even by subscribing for its stock.

Nor was this all. Not only had credit to be created for the enterprise against all these difficulties, but when money was raised, the material for the road—the iron, the spikes, the tools to dig, the powder to blast, the locomotives, the cars, the machinery, everything—had to be shipped from New York around Cape Horn, to make an expensive and hazardous eight months' voyage, before it could be landed in San Francisco, and had then to be reshipped one hundred and twenty miles to Sacramento by water. Not a foot of iron was laid on the road on all the eight hundred miles to Ogden, not a spike was driven, not a dirt-car was moved, nor a powder-blast set off, that was not first brought around Cape Horn; and at every step of its progress the work depended upon the promptness with which all this material was shipped for a sea-voyage of thousands of miles.

Men, too, as well as material, had to be obtained from a great distance. California, thinly populated, with wages very high at that time, could not supply the force needed. Laborers were obtained from New York, from the lower country, and finally ten thousand Chinese were brought over the Pacific Ocean, and their patient toil completed the work.

When you get to Sacramento, if you have a quarter of an hour to spare, ask somebody to show you No. 54 K Street. It is not far from the railroad depot, and it is the place where the Central Pacific Railroad was nursed, and from which it grew. You will see over the plain frame store a weather-beaten old sign, "Huntington and Hopkins," and if you walk in you will find a complete assortment of hardware and metals. Here C. P. Huntington and Mark Hopkins, the first from Connecticut, the last from the hill country of Massachusetts, gathered, by diligence, shrewdness, and honest dealing, a respectable fortune. They were so cautious that they never owned a dollar of stock in a mine, never had a branch house, never sent out a "drummer" to get business, and never sued a man for a debt.

SNOW-SHEDS ON THE CENTRAL PACIFIC RAILROAD.

It is still related in Sacramento that the cardinal rule of the firm was to ask a high price for everything, but to sell only a good article—the best in the market.

In fact, Huntington and Hopkins were merchants, and nothing else, in business. They sold hardware. But in politics they were Free-soilers,

INTERIOR OF SNOW-SHED, CENTRAL PACIFIC RAILROAD.

and later Republicans, and they did not sell their principles. It came about that No. 54 K Street became a place where leading Republicans met to discuss the news and plan opposition to the Democratic party, which then, in 1856–'58, though probably numerically the weakest, was strongest in money, in its aggressive spirit, and in social influence in the State. In those early days, when a Pacific Railroad, though talked of, was still a dream of the far-off future, "54 K Street," which later for some years found room for all the various offices of the Central Pacific Company, without disturbing the hardware business—in those days it accommodated in a modest upper-story room the first Republican press of California. This was called the *Times;* it supported Fremont; and Mr. Cole, afterward United States Senator from California, was its editor. Thus, "54

K Street" was the head-quarters of the Republicans in the northern and central parts of the State; and here met, with Huntington and Hopkins among others, Stanford, afterward Governor of the State and President of the Central Pacific Company, and the Crockers.

Sitting around the stove on dull winter evenings in the store at 54 K Street, the two hardware merchants and their Republican allies, Stanford and the Crockers, when politics flagged, are said to have returned again and again to the project of a Pacific road. The desire for a road was in everybody's mind in California; the question entered so completely into politics that no man for years could hope to be chosen to an office by either party unless he was believed to be the zealous friend of a transcontinental road.

In 1850-'51 a wagon road was the most that was hoped for; and to this everybody subscribed as he was able. Then came the telegraph; and in that all public-spirited men took stock, or to it they gave outright what they could spare. Meantime, year after year, the Pacific Railroad Bill appeared in Congress, was discussed, and laid over. The "snow-capped Sierras" were the bugbear of Senators; but Republicans in California thought they saw in this only a pretence, when they heard Democratic politicians proposing to divide the State into two, and make two Pacific railroads—one for the North and one for the South.

Finally there came, to build the little Sacramento Valley Railroad, one Judah, an engineer, who, many people thought, was Pacific Railroad crazy. He begged some money among the most sanguine railroad men, and made a reconnoissance of two or three gaps in the Sierra. After some time he proclaimed that he had discovered what everybody wished for—a possible passage for a railroad. By way of Dutch Flat, he asserted, there was a long, easy ascent, practicable for a road. Judah, sanguine and restless, personally solicited subscriptions from the people of Dutch Flat, Auburn, Grass Valley, and Sacramento, to help him to make a more thorough exploration. Public meetings were held, and men gave, according to their means, ten, fifty, a hundred dollars for this object. A law of the State, which made every stockholder individually liable for the debts of a company, then made people cautious about subscribing to new projects, and Judah got his support chiefly in gifts; and among his leading supporters in this way were the five merchants I have named.

About this time came the rumble of approaching war, and the San Francisco capitalists, mostly at that time Southern men, would not have anything more to do with the scheme; and once more it seemed to be crushed.

Working under the State laws, which provided that before a company could have a charter $1000 must be paid in for every mile of its proposed road, it was not easy to raise the capital—about $135,000—needed to obtain a charter; and yet affairs had now come to such a pass that it was no longer worth while, or even possible, to go on without organization. Sacramento was canvassed, but with too little success; San Francisco had buttoned up its pockets; and at last Huntington, who had refused to give any more money for mere reconnoissances, proposed to half a dozen others to undertake the enterprise among themselves of making a regular and careful survey. "I'll be one of ten, or one of eight, to bear the whole expense, if Hopkins will consent," he said, at a meeting called at Governor Stanford's house; and thus the great work was at last begun, seven men binding themselves in a compact for three years to pay all needful expenses of a thorough survey out of their own pockets. Of these seven, one, Judah, had no means, and shortly afterward died, and another presently dropped out. There were a few outside subscriptions; but it is curious to remember that when a prominent banker friendly to the project, and having faith in it, was asked to take some stock, he declined on the plea that the credit of his bank would suffer if he were known to be connected with so wild a scheme. This was in 1860, only twenty-one years ago.

The Central Pacific Railroad Company was thus at last organized, with Leland Stanford as president, C. P. Huntington as vice-president, and Mark Hopkins as secretary and treasurer; and the same men hold the same places to-day, with the exception of Mark Hopkins, who is dead.

Affairs now began to look, to the prudent hardware dealers at No. 54 K Street, as though they were likely to have more railroad presently than would be good for the hardware business. While the explorations and surveys were going on in the winter of 1860-'61, and while a Pacific Railroad Bill was getting drawn in Congress, business details began to be examined; and at 54 K Street they asked themselves why it was that so few railroads in this country had been successful in first hands. The answer was that, first, they were not prudently and economically managed in the beginning; and, second, that American railroads are built largely on credit: thus it almost always happens that the interest account begins to run before the road can earn money; and to pay interest when no business is done would ruin almost any undertaking, even the hardware business, thought these shrewd merchants.

As to the first fault—on the following page is a picture of the first building erected by the Central Pacific Railroad Company. You will notice, perhaps, that "C. P. Huntington"—*Central Pacific* Huntington he began to be called in those days—was its "architect." The engineer had designed what to his professional eye seemed a proper building for the Sacramento business. It was large, elaborate, complete, and would have cost $12,000. Huntington approved of the plan, which he said was *admirable for by-and-by*. "For the present," said he, "we are not doing much business, and *this* would do better;" and with a piece of chalk he drew the outline, on one of the iron doors of 54 K Street, of such a board structure as he thought sufficient; the four sides were nailed together in an afternoon; it was roofed the next day; it cost $150; and when it grew too small for its original uses, it was removed and used as a paint shop. There was no nonsense or flummery about 54 K Street. And I may add that the same spirit still prevails there. Of course the company now owns and occupies an extensive river frontage in Sacramento, as well as in Oakland, at Vallejo, and in San Francisco, for its business; its real estate is worth many millions of dollars; but the business offices are in very plain quarters in San Francisco, and if you visit the New York office, you will find there an equally plain establishment.

FIRST OFFICE OF THE CENTRAL PACIFIC RAILROAD.

As to the second point—Huntington was, after consultation, sent to Washington, strictly enjoined to see that in the Pacific Railroad Bill it should be provided that the company should pay no interest on the bonds it received of the Government for at least ten years; and if this condition was refused, to abandon the whole matter, and sell the wreck for what it would bring.

Another and more notable thing these five men did. When they sent Huntington to Washington, they gave him a power of attorney authorizing him to do for them and in their name anything whatever—to buy, sell, bargain, convey, borrow, or lend, without any *if* or *but*, let or hinderance whatever, except that he should fare alike with them, in all that concerned their great project. It is not often that five middle-aged business men are found to place such entire confidence in each other as this; but it was vital to their success that they should feel and act just thus.

At last, one day, Huntington telegraphed from Washington: "The bill has passed, and we have drawn the elephant." Thereupon the company accepted the conditions, and opened books for stock subscriptions to the amount of eight and a half millions to carry the road to the State line. The beginning was not hopeful. The rich men of San Francisco did not subscribe a cent. One man in Nevada took one share. Others elsewhere took five one-hundred-dollar shares more. Six hundred dollars in all were subscribed at the first rush to build the Central Pacific Railroad! Later, mechanics, working-women, notably one public-spirited woman, and others in Sacramento and other small towns—homesick people who wanted to get back to the Atlantic States without the perils of the sea, it was said—took up about one hundred and fifty shares more. It was a long time before more than a million and a half of stock was taken.

Meantime, in the summer of 1861 a considerable traffic had sprung up between Nevada and Sacramento. This was done over the Placerville Turnpike, and Mark Hopkins took pains to ascertain the amount and value of this commerce, which the Pacific Railroad would do, of course, as soon as it was sufficiently completed. He caused the number of teams on the turnpike and the number of passengers to be counted; and this gave a certain promise of local business. Next it was necessary to cause well-known bankers to certify to the world the good standing and pecuniary responsibility of the principal subscribers to the stock. The California Legislature then merged the State charter in the Federal charter; all the statutes of the State bearing upon the company were gathered together; and thus armed with facts and credentials, Huntington went to New York—to raise a great many millions of dollars.

He was promptly told by capitalists that the bonds of the company had no value in their eyes until some part of the road had been built. The Government bonds were, at that stage, not to be given until forty miles of the road was completed. The stock subscriptions came in too slowly for practical purposes. Huntington, courageous, full of resources, and of faith in what he had undertaken to do, announced that he would not sell his bonds except for money, and that he would not sell any unless a million and a half were taken; and finally, when that amount was bid for, he called all the bidders together, explained in detail the full importance and value of the enterprise, and thereupon the bonds were taken, on the condition that Huntington and his four partners—Hopkins, Stanford, and the two Crockers—should make themselves personally responsible for the money received, until the bonds could be exchanged for Government bonds. Huntington did not hesitate a moment to pledge his own moderate fortune and those of his associates to this effect. These bonds built thirty-one miles of the road—the easiest part of it, fortunately.

And now came the severest test of the courage and endurance of the men at 54 K Street. Eleven months passed over before they could get the Government bonds for the completed and accepted part of the line; these bonds in the mean time had gone down from one and a half per cent. premium in gold, where they stood when the charter was accepted, as low as thirty-nine cents for the dollar. Railroad iron in the same period went up from $50 to $135 per ton. All other materials, locomotives, etc., rose in the same proportion; insurance for the eight or nine months' voyage around Cape Horn, which every pound of the material of the road-bed and running stock had to make, rose from two and a half to ten per cent., by reason of the rebel cruisers; freights from $18 to $45 per ton.

Intent on keeping down the interest account, the five men at 54 K Street asked the State to pay for twenty years the interest on a million and a half of bonds, in exchange for which they gave a valuable granite quarry, guaranteed free transportation of all stone from it for the public buildings of the State, and also free transportation over their line of all State troops, criminals, lunatics, and paupers. This was done. Then Sacramento and some of the counties were asked to exchange their bonds for the stock of the company, and this was done by a popular vote. But most of these contracts had to be enforced afterward in the courts.

Meantime the money was used up. The business was from the first kept rigidly under control; every contract was made terminable at the option of the company; every hand employed was paid off monthly; and in reading over some old contracts I came upon a clause specially obliging the contractors to keep liquor out of the camps. When Huntington, after long and trying labors in New York, returned to Sacramento, he found the treasure-chest so low that it was necessary to diminish the laboring force, or at once raise more means. "Huntington and Hopkins," said he, "can, out of their own means, pay five hundred men during a year; how many can each of you keep on the line?" The five men agreed in council at 54 K Street that out of their own private fortunes they would maintain and pay eight hundred men during a year on the road.

That resolution ended their troubles. Before the year was over they had received their Government bonds. They still had the worst and most costly part of the line to build; they still had to transport all their material around Cape Horn; they had many trials, difficulties, and obstacles before them, for nearly four years were consumed in crossing the Sierra; they had to encounter lawsuits, opposition, ridicule, evil prophecies, losses;

had to organize a vast laboring force, drill long tunnels, shovel away in one spring sixty feet of snow over seven miles of the line, merely to get at the road-bed; had to set up saw-mills by the dozen in the mountains to saw ties; haul half a dozen locomotives and twenty tons of iron twenty-six miles over the mountains by ox-teams; haul water forty and wood twenty miles for the construction trains on the alkali plains; but it seems to me that this brave resolution was the turning-point in their enterprise. Surely there is something admirable in the courage of five country merchants, ignorant of railroad building, and unknown to the world, assuming such a load as the support of eight hundred men for a year out of their own pockets for an enterprise in the success of which, in their hands, very few of their own friends believed.

The secret of their success was, that these five country merchants meant in good faith to build a railroad. They did not expect to get

ALKALI DESERT, CENTRAL PACIFIC RAILROAD.

money out of an enterprise before they had put money of their own into it. They managed all the details as carefully and prudently as they were accustomed to manage the hardware or dry-goods business. They were honest men. When Huntington began to buy iron and machinery in New York, people flocked to him to sell, and there is a story of some one who came with an offer of a handsome commission to Huntington if he would deal with him. "I want all the commissions I can get," was the reply; "*but I want them put in the bill. This* road has got to be built without any stealings."

"Don't keep a man at work whom you can't pay regularly at the end of the month: we won't stop work, but if we can pay only one man, we will employ only one," was their rule. Therefore every contract was made terminable at the will of the company. In New York, where the money was to be raised on the bonds, and the material had to be bought and shipped, the bonds were sold only for money, and the iron bought for cash. And all this time the interest was kept down by every possible care and prevision. "If there is any money to be made in building this road," said Huntington, "I mean that the company shall make it." When somebody tells you that "the Central Pacific people were close," you will understand that they were honest.

Nor were they satisfied merely to complete their road. They have busied themselves in establishing feeders for it in California, and already own and manage almost the whole railroad system of that State. North toward Oregon, and southward, through the great San Joaquin Valley, to Los Angeles, San Bernardino, the Colorado River through Arizona and part of New Mexico, they have opened a vast region by a new transcontinental road. The California and Oregon Railroad opens the whole of the great Sacramento Valley and the northern part of the State, and connects with the Oregon Railroad system. The Southern Pacific Railroad, with the Visalia and other branches, in like manner opens up the still richer San Joaquin Valley, as well as the series of smaller valleys lying west of the Coast Range, which already produce enormous crops of grain. The Western Pacific and California Pacific Railroads complete connections between Sacramento and San Francisco; and the Napa Valley, the Copperopolis, the San José, Watsonville, Monterey, and other branch roads gather in the products of fertile regions, and carry them to the main lines.

The Central Pacific Railroad was one of the most expensive to build in the world. Its engineers, Montague and Gray, would have been famous all over the world had they constructed a road half as difficult in Europe.*

---

* S. S. Montague, still chief engineer of the Central Pacific Railroad, was the active and working head of the engineer corps which built the road. He was born in New Hampshire, but was brought to Illinois by his parents when he was but six years old, in the year 1836. He attended the country schools in his neighborhood, and at the age of twenty-two, having shown readiness in mathematical studies, joined a corps of railroad engineers and learned his profession in the field, in the States of Illinois and Iowa. He lived on his father's farm until he was twenty years of age, attending school during the winter, and taught school for one year, after he was twenty. In 1859 he left home to seek his fortune at Pike's Peak; but the company with which he travelled broke up, and he joined another going across the plains to California, and there found work on the Folsom and Sacramento Railroad, which was then building. In 1862 he joined Theodore Judah, as his first assistant on the Central Pacific. Judah died in 1863, and Montague succeeded him as chief engineer in this great undertaking. He had to locate the greater part of the line, and to organize

C. P. HUNTINGTON.

They had not only to build a road through an almost inaccessible country,

and command the force which built the road; and though the difficulties he had to contend with are apparent even to laymen, only professional engineers, conversant with the work, can, I suspect, appreciate its magnitude, and the many novel questions presenting themselves in its execution.

Colonel George E. Gray, consulting engineer during the progress of the work, was born in Oneida County, New York; began his career as an engineer on the State canals in 1839, and was engaged on different railroads in New York till 1853. In that year he became chief engineer of the New York Central Railroad, where he remained till May, 1865, when he came to California as consulting engineer of the Central Pacific Company. He built the first wrought-iron bridge on the New York Central Railway. Colonel Grey has added to his renown as an engineer later by building the Southern Pacific Railroad, on which there are several unique and daring engineering feats, such as the "Loop," before described.

but when it was completed they had the farther problem of running trains over it at all seasons. You will see little of the costly and solid snow-sheds, through which you pass mostly by night, and, which are now being roofed with iron; you will not see at all, perhaps, the ponderous snow-ploughs, of various patterns, some to push the snow off on one side, some on the other, down a precipice; others made merely to fling it off the track on the plains; and behind which, during the winter, often eight heavy engines were harnessed to "buck" the snow, and throw it from twenty to sixty feet away.

Nor will you see, unless you inquire for it, in Sacramento, an admirable institution, the Central Pacific Railroad Hospital, a fine building, which stands in an open square, cost $60,000, and is in part supported by a monthly contribution of fifty cents from every man engaged with the company, from the President down. One of the ablest physicians of Sacramento has charge of this hospital, and he too was one of eight men who, in 1856, originated the Republican party in California. In the report of the State Board of Health this hospital is spoken of as "first in the order of salubrity and successful results in the world," and it is in every way a complete and carefully managed institution.

The company now employs more men than all the other manufacturers in California; its pay-roll in the State alone contains nearly seven thousand names. It manufactures within the State most of the articles and material used in building or running its roads; it has the most complete land-office in the United States, not excepting that at Washington— a place where you may select on maps, locate, and pay for, any quantity of the company's lands you wish for, and where you may obtain in a few minutes detailed and specific information concerning lands in any part of California.

One incident of the building of the road will conclude what I have to say of it. In April, 1869, ten miles of road were built in one day. This is probably the greatest feat of railroad building on record. What is most remarkable about it is that eight men handled all the iron on this ten miles. These eight giants walked ten miles that day, and lifted and handled one thousand tons of rail bars each.

Since the completion of the Central Pacific road the same men have built the Southern Pacific, and have overcome in that enterprise engineering and other difficulties fully as great as those encountered in their first undertaking.

ROUNDING CAPE HORN.

CHAPTER III.

THE TOURIST IN CALIFORNIA.—WHAT TO SEE, AND HOW TO SEE IT.

THE tourist will find San Francisco itself one of the pleasantest and most novel of all the sights of California. The hotels are for the most part admirably kept; the streets are full of strange sights; the Cliff House will make one of your pleasantest experiences; at Woodward's Gardens a good collection of grizzly bears, and other wild beasts native to California, and an admirable aquarium, will amuse and instruct children from fifteen to fifty years of age; the Chinese and Japanese shops have curiosities at all prices, from twenty-five cents to five hundred dollars;

and the Chinese quarter will occupy your leisure several days, if you are at all curious.

Your first drive in San Francisco is likely to be to the Cliff House. You may breakfast there if you like; and as all out-door amusements in San Francisco are controlled by the climate during the spring and summer months, the cold sea-breeze making the afternoons uncomfortable, it is a pretty and sensible thing to rise at six or seven some morning, and see the sea-lions while it is yet warm and still. Moreover, you are sure of a good breakfast at the Cliff House, and you take it on the veranda, with all China and Japan, and the King of the Cannibal Islands, looking at you across the broad Pacific.

If you have children in your party, they will not tire of watching the sea-lions, no matter how long you stay. And if you have any fancy yourself in wild beasts, you will be both amazed and amused at the huge, strange creatures which cover the rocks two hundred yards from you, and look, with their pointed heads and shiny bodies, like monstrous maggots crawling and squirming; who lie like dead things upon the rocks; whose howls and hoarse, discordant roars reach to you and make strange music to your meal. A seal in Barnum's Museum was a strange beast—but these monstrous, misshapen creatures, furious, wild, free, yawning in your face, pushing each other aside, quarrelling, suckling their young, rolling off the precipitous rocks into the sea, make the strangest sight my eyes ever beheld. If Gustave Doré could see them, he would add another weird picture to his chamber of horrors.

The greater part of San Francisco is smoothly laid with wooden pavement; and the city is approached from every side over admirable roads. A New Yorker boasts of Central Park roads till he has driven thirty miles in a brief forenoon, forty or fifty miles in a day, here over the best ways I ever saw. Go where you will within fifty miles of the city, and you find smooth, hard roads, broad avenues, often, as at Santa Clara, lined with long, double rows of fine shade-trees—roads over which you may drive at the rate of ten or twelve miles per hour and do no harm to your horses nor tire yourself.

You will easily find the streets in San Francisco devoted to the Chinese. They occupy a considerable part of the heart of the city; and their shops, in Sacramento, Dupont, and other streets, are open to visitors, though you will not find much to buy in them, nor many of the merchants and clerks able to speak or understand English. Ladies and children may safely and properly walk in the main streets of the Chinese quarter by day. The tourist who wishes to investigate farther should

THE SENTINEL, YOSEMITE VALLEY.

get a policeman stationed among the Chinese to show him around after dark. He will see some strange and unpleasant sights; and ladies and children must be excluded from this tour. But all may go to the Chinese theatre. If you have a party of ladies and children you should apply the day before to the manager of the theatre, a Chinaman, whom you will find on the premises, for a box. This will cost you three dollars, and fifty cents additional for every person in your party. Go about half-past eight, and stay until ten or eleven. The boxes are up-stairs, at one end of the gallery; opposite you will see the Chinese women huddled together in a place by themselves; the audience below vehemently resents the indecorum of a woman appearing in the pit. The play often contains some admirable feats of tumbling; but the whole performance you will find most strange and extraordinary.

What it is like I will try to tell you. What the play I saw meant I cannot tell you, of course, but it was evidently well done; for it was easy to see that the audience enjoyed it. Once in a great while the clown extorted a laugh; once in a while the women, in the place set apart for them, wiped their eyes; meantime, the person who answers to the peanut man in our Bowery went his slow round, with a big basket of oranges and sweetmeats on his head; the audience lit its cigars and smoked; men passed silently in and out; but not a cat-call, not a noise of any kind disturbed the harmony; not a curious look even toward our private-box, where sat ladies and children who must have been objects of curiosity to them.

The auditorium is built like that of any common theatre. It has a large pit, and above that a gallery, at one end of which are several private boxes, while at the other end is a space closed off for the Chinese women, who do not sit with the men. The whole is without ornament, and has a squalid look, as though it had been poorly done and was now poorly kept. Yet our box was clean. The chairs were very ordinary; but the place had been swept, and was not greasy.

As for the stage—attend, and I will try to describe it. In the first place, the orchestra sit at the back of the stage; they play vigorously and continuously, now on stringed instruments, which give out an ear-piercing sound like a multitude of insane bagpipes, now on cymbals, small gongs, and various other atrocious devices to make a worse and less endurable noise than the fiddles. I never heard such an outrageous collocation of sounds in my life; and how the musicians themselves endure it I don't know.

Before these gentlemen, playing in their shirt-sleeves, taking tea occasionally, and smoking when they chose—one absurd creature sawed away in his shirt-sleeves at his fiddle for dear life, sucking meanwhile the end of a very long pipe, which he had to hold out in the air by stretching his head back—before this wonderful orchestra, which kept better time than many orchestras I have heard in opera-houses, the play went on. There are no curtains nor scenes. At the left side is an entrance, and at the other an exit-way, each draped with a flap of cloth, through which the players dash at a trot. The properties to be used in the play stand at the sides of the stage, and the men who are to bring on or carry off these pieces of furniture lounge about among them, or pass back and forth from behind the screen which conceals the greenroom. They are very dexterous in placing or removing their properties, and manage to keep out of the way of the players. At one side, in the screen, is a square hole, at which you see the nose and eyes of the stage-manager occasionally, directing.

Everything is cheap, squalid, and, to our eyes, disreputable. But the players, who came on in the cheap magnificence of players everywhere, were in earnest apparently, and shrieked, and gesticulated, and sung with what seemed to me the careful and studied precision of men doing their best.

By-the-way, the Chinaman, who has naturally a deep and pleasant voice, no sooner appears on the stage than every utterance is in a shrill falsetto, which is more like vehement caterwauling than any other sound I remember to have heard. When we got home from the theatre one of my children made a door to creak in the room, and we all burst out laughing as we recognized the most impassioned tones of the chief actor in the play—or part of a play—we had just heard.

There is something dry and overstrained in their attitudes, gestures, and tones. It is as though they had been refining and refining for centuries, until at last they had got every natural tone and movement off their stage, and made it just what Hamlet did not want it to be. The mincing pronunciation which he counselled his players to avoid these have made the object of their lives. Not one of the players—not even the clown—was for an instant betrayed into a movement or tone of voice proper and natural to him or any other human being; and after we had sat for an hour, listening and looking, we could not help but admire the atrocious perfection of their unnaturalness.

The first part of the play we saw was what we should call an opera: that is to say, the dialogue was sung to the accompaniment of music. The "music" was ear-piercing, shrill, loud, and to our ears only a horrible discord. But there was evidently a method in it; the leader, whose instrument consisted of two ivory sticks, with which he beat very audible time on a block of iron, had his shirt-sleeved orchestra under full control; and the singers and the players all kept admirable time. The singing was, of course, as unnatural as the playing; and when the chief personage of the piece, a high mandarin, dressed gorgeously, and with peacock feathers a yard long sticking out of his crown, attempted a quaver or trill, we all in our box burst into uncontrollable laughter.

The action goes on continuously; the players every two or three minutes rush off the stage, only to rush on again at the other entrance: in some parts of the play there were at least twenty characters crowded on the narrow stage; and it was very droll to see the king, when he was for a moment disengaged, turn his back on the audience and take a swig of tea out of a teapot which stood handy; or, when he had for some stage purpose removed his crown, turn his back on the audience and carefully replace it before a small looking-glass, held up before him by one of the "supernumeraries."

In one part of the play there was some excellent tumbling; and in another two of the characters took the part of the lion, being assisted by a huge pasteboard lion's head, or what in China they imagine a lion's

EAGLE GAP, ON THE TRUCKEE RIVER.

head to be like, with a lower jaw of brass, which was made to clap noisily, to the terror of the players. The body consisted of a silk cloth, in which a small boy was hidden, who represented the lion's hinder extremities and got a contemptuous kick on one occasion from the clown. These trappings hung openly on a nail at the side of the stage, and were taken down in the middle of the play by a fellow who gravely climbed up on a ladder to reach it.

There was no applause, no cheering, no noisy manifestation of displeasure or delight; there is no bar-room in the theatre; the manager and lessee sat decorously on the back of a seat among the audience, smoking his cigar; and the play was to last until two o'clock A.M., being given to a numerous audience, who, I was told, paid thirty cents per head to see it—and no free list.

You should also, during the day, visit the Chinese temples or josshouses, to which a policeman will guide you. They are in the shabby style of the theatre, decorated with cheap tinsel; but you will see the Chinese manner of worship, and in one of the temples some curious carving in wood.

The Chinese quarter is perfectly safe and orderly; and you need no protection, even for ladies and children, in going to the theatre or elsewhere.

Among the sights in California most attractive to the tourist, the groves of Big Trees and the wonderful Yosemite Valley are, of course, the chief.

Travellers who come for but a hurried stay will economize time by seeing first San Francisco and its neighborhood, in which I include the San José Valley, the Almaden mine, Monterey, where there is now a splendid hotel, making the sunny old town a justly favorite wateringplace; and Santa Cruz; and on the north the Geysers (Clear Lake if you have time), the Napa Valley, Santa Rosa, and the Sonoma country. Having "done" the coast, you can turn your face eastward, and begin the tour of the Trees and the Valley.

To the Geysers you should go by way of Vallejo and Calistoga, returning by way of Cloverdale and San Quentin. Thus you will see on the way the Napa Valley and the curious country about Calistoga, with its petrified forest and warm springs, and on your return Santa Rosa, Petaluma, the Sonoma Valley, and San Rafael, one of the pleasantest sheltered nooks on the whole coast.

In going to the Geysers you have an exciting but not dangerous ride through a fine country. The horses are well trained, and the drivers are experienced men. The great whips on this route usually drive six-in-hand; and if you sit on the box you will find yourself whirled around turns so short that sometimes you lose sight of the ears of the leaders. The road, which for miles skirts a precipice, is well-built and carefully looked after; no accident has ever happened, and you may safely trust yourself to the drivers. At the Geysers, where there is a comfortable hotel, you arrive in the afternoon, and you leave the next morning. Do not omit to take a soda bath. It is very refreshing, and itself worth the journey.

You buy your tickets for the round trip in San Francisco. It should be understood that the so-called Geysers are not spouting springs. A narrow valley, or cañon as it is called in California, is filled with flowing hot springs, and the whole soil is covered with a crust of sulphur, iron-rust, and other mineral deposits, and filled with steam from boiling water. The surface of the ground is so hot that you will be uncomfortable in walking over it if you wear thin-soled shoes.

South of San Francisco, the San José Valley contains the finest country places on the Pacific slope. The best way to see it is to telegraph beforehand for a carriage to await you at San Mateo, and tell the driver to show you the best parts of the country, and set you off at Mayfield in time to catch the evening train for San José. There you will find the Auzeray House very comfortable. Engage a team overnight to convey you the next morning to the New Almaden quicksilver mines. Set off at half-past seven, and you will have time to see the works, return to dinner, and drive after dinner to Santa Clara over the beautiful road called the Alameda, which is shaded for two or three miles by the finest trees of their kind in California.

From Santa Clara, or San José if you return thither, the train will take you, by way of Gilroy, to Watsonville, where you may see wheat growing luxuriantly almost to the sea-shore; and through a charming country to Santa Cruz, one of the pleasantest watering-places of California, and to Monterey, the old capital of California. Monterey has become of late the most famous and one of the pleasantest sea-side resorts in California. The old Spanish town has lain asleep until within a year or two, inaccessible except by stage or private conveyance, until now it is reached by railroad in four hours from San Francisco, and a really magnificent hotel accommodates luxuriously a multitude of visitors. The climate of Monterey is very sunny and pleasant, and will be a relief to you after you have spent some days in San Francisco, where the afternoon gales are harsh during the summer and fall.

The excursion to San José, Monterey, and Santa Cruz is one of the most delightful to be made around San Francisco, and it will give you an excellent example of the agricultural wealth of California, as well as of the picturesque beauty of its scenery. In May and June the whole country is covered with lovely flowers. The brilliant yellow and orange of the escholtzia, or California poppy, and the tender blue and white of the lupine, line the road and cover the fields in broad masses, which give a perpetual delight to the eye.

The oak groves, too, will excite your admiration. The California oak

THE THREE BROTHERS, YOSEMITE VALLEY.

is a low-branching and far-spreading tree, disposed in irregular masses, which give a lovely, park-like effect to the landscape, and add very much to the rural beauty of this part of the country. The roses, too, grow in masses, free from disease, and of a size and depth of color not found with us in the East; and in the highly cultivated places in the San José Valley you will meet with the pomegranate, the fig, the almond, and a great variety of flowering shrubs, and some evergreens, unknown to us in the East, many of the former brought from Japan, China, and Australia. The eucalyptus, or Australian gum, is deservedly a favorite tree in all parts of California; it has made, in favorable places, a growth of fifteen feet in a single season, is evergreen, and its bluish-green foliage contrasts finely with such trees as the lovely Monterey cypress, which is also a rapid grower.

The camellia here remains out-of-doors all winter; the heliotrope is a stout, woody shrub; the gladiolus is already past its bloom in June, and is planted in the fall; and you find it difficult to recognize in the massive eight-foot-high shrub, whose brilliant bloom almost hides its foliage, and which is used as a hedge or screen, the scarlet geranium. Even the humble little sweet alyssum, which with us creeps along the ground, here rears its flower-spikes two feet high.

The windmills are a peculiar feature of the Californian landscape. You see them even in San Francisco, on the tops of houses; but in the suburbs every place has one. Everywhere ample provision is made for water; and on some country places miles of water-pipes are laid for watering lawns and flowers.

Field irrigation is not practised near San Francisco except in special cases; but during the long dry season, which lasts from April to October, when it does not rain at all, they preserve their lawns by sprinkling, and new plantations are also freely watered. Artesian wells are common; and the windmill stands usually on top of a tank, from which the water is distributed to the house, the stables, and all over the grounds, hydrants being placed at frequent intervals. From the hydrant a hose is led to a sprinkler, which stands on the lawn, on a tripod, and sends out constantly a thin and finely divided spray. The gardener moves this from time to time, and thus the whole spacious lawn is watered and kept as green and lovely as though it were in the White Mountains.

With such help, I need not tell you that the strawberry grows to perfection. It is larger and, I think, much sweeter than with us. I am not, at home, a strawberry lover, but here I have relished it without sugar. On one place, near Santa Clara, I noticed an ingenious arrangement for irrigating a strawberry bed of about three acres. A large, shallow tank stood near one end of this " patch," with its bottom nearly on a level with the upper end of the rows. From this was led a main, which was connected with a pipe running across the whole upper end of the great field. Between every two of the rows a hole was made in this pipe, and this hole was stopped with a wooden plug. Thus we saw only a long row of wooden plugs; pull out any one of these, and the water began immediately to run down the depression between the two rows.

Of course all this appliance of windmills, water-pipes, tanks, and fountains is possible only in a country where they have steady winds and no severe frosts. With us the tanks would burst, the pipes would have to be deeply buried in the ground; and the whole machinery would be continually getting out of order. Yet I could not help seeing that our common complaint of rusty and unpleasing lawns during July and August could be prevented, on the fine places near New York, by the help of a windmill, and a tank, which might be emptied in the fall and housed over.

The Californians seem to me to enjoy all the advantages of a tropical climate with but a few of its disadvantages. They have about here no

THE GEYSERS.

malarious fevers, no mosquitoes, no poisonous reptiles; yet their roses bloom all the year round. "I do not know the day in the whole year when I cannot gather a bouquet in my garden," said a San Francisco lady to me. In one place in Oakland I saw the gas-meter out-of-doors, near the stable; dwellings need no furnaces to warm them in winter; and the whole cumbrous machinery by which we guard ourselves and our animals and tender plants against cold is here unknown. The greenhouse and conservatory are only affectations; the oleander remains in the ground the winter through, and the fan-palm flourishes everywhere.

The people of San Francisco complain of their climate, which is, in truth, somewhat harsh. Every day at eleven o'clock during the summer they get a stiff and cool sea-breeze. If you go out in the morning, no matter how warm it is, you are warned to take with you a shawl or overcoat. But, on the other hand, for seven months in the year you may lock up your umbrella; and we, too, have dusty roads, but no constant alleviation of cool breezes.

Moreover, a journey of thirty miles puts you into an entirely different climate. The San José Valley, the Napa Valley, and others, lie behind the Coast Range, and are thus sheltered from the ocean breezes; and here there is no afternoon gale, and all the winds are gentle. We came up from San José on a brilliant, warm day, which we had enjoyed by driving early to the quicksilver mines, and later over the lovely Alameda to Santa Clara. As the train neared the city we closed the windows; presently the ladies drew shawls about them; and, when we got out of the cars at San Francisco, I drew on my overcoat, and was glad to close the carriage windows; and we sat by a fire in the evening. Thus it is all summer; and as there is no rain, the country, of course, gets dusty; and in the country houses you find wraps for the neck, and other appliances, to keep out the dust when you drive out, and in your room a queer sprinkler over the wash-basin, wherewith conveniently to wash the dust out of your hair when you return from a drive.

YOSEMITE FALLS.

Since the earlier editions of this book were published the extension of the railroad system in California and the completion of stage-roads to difficult points have made great changes, favorable to the convenience of the tourist. Thus one has no longer to ride on horseback into the Yosemite; one need no longer make a tedious sea-voyage to visit Santa Barbara, Los Angeles, and San Diego; much time is saved, as well as some expense, and much weariness to ladies and children. To reach the Yosemite Valley, it was formerly necessary to take a long stage ride of three days and a difficult horseback ride. Now you go by rail to Madera, on the Southern

SOUTH DOME, YOSEMITE VALLEY.

Pacific Railroad, seven hours from San Francisco, by stage thence to Clark's, near the Mariposa grove of Big Trees, where you sleep the second night; and thence by stage still, a short drive to your hotel in the valley.

It is a pity to "do" this excursion in haste. You should give ten days to it, at least; though you can be back at Madera in six days from the time you left San Francisco, and still have spent two whole days in the valley, and half a day among the Big Trees, in the Mariposa grove. But nowhere else on your tour will you so much regret haste as in your visit to the Yosemite and the Big Trees.

You leave your trunks at Madera, and take with you only a change of clothing; and you should wear stout shoes and a broad-brimmed hat, and take with you shawls and a light overcoat. In the valley there are numerous charming excursions, and guides and safe horses for them all.

A business man or a statistician would tell you, in a few words, that the Yosemite Valley is a floor eight miles long by two wide, with walls three-quarters of a mile high. He would give you, farther, the following figures concerning the height of the precipitous mountains which form the walls, and of the water-falls which give variety to the wonderful scene:

MOUNTAINS.

Indian Name.	Signification.	American Name.	Height.
To-tock-a-nu-la	Great Chief of the Valley	El Capitan	3300 feet.
Poo-see-nah Chuck-ka	Large Acorn Cache	Cathedral Rocks	2660 "
		The Cathedral Spires	1800 "
Pom-pom-pasus	Mountains Playing Leap-frog	Three Brothers	3830 "
Hep-se-tuck-a-nah	Gone in	Union Rocks	3500 "
Loya	Signal Station	Sentinel Rock	3043 "
Loya	Signal Station	Sentinel Dome	4500 "
Ummo	Lost Arrow		3000 "
Patillima		Glacier Rock	3200 "
To-coy-ae	Shade to Indian Baby Basket	Royal Arches	1800 "
Hunto	The Watching Eye	Washington Column	1875 "
		North Dome	3568 "
Tis-sa-ack	Goddess of the Valley	South Dome	4737 "
Wayan	Pine Mountain	Mount Watkins	3900 "
	Cloud's Rest		6034 "
	Cap of Liberty		4000 "
	Mount Star King		5600 "

WATER-FALLS.

		Cataract	900 feet.
Po-ho-no	Night Wind	Bridal Veil	630 "
Yo-semite	Large Grizzly Bear	Yosemite	2634 "
	First Fall		1600 "
	Second Fall		600 "
	Third Fall		434 "
Py-wy-ack	Sparkling Water	Vernal	350 "
Yo-wy-ye		Nevada	700 "
Illilouette	The Beautiful	South Fork	600 "
Yo-coy-ae	Shade to Indian Baby Basket	Royal Arch Falls	1000 "
Loya		Sentinel Falls	3000 "

He would add, for purposes of comparison, that 5280 feet make a mile; that the great fall of Niagara is but 163 feet high; and that the precipitous Palisades of the Hudson River are, at their highest point, less than 600 feet high.

There the statistician would leave you; and he would be right. No man can so describe the Yosemite Valley as to give to one who has not seen it even a faint idea of its wonderful, strange, and magnificent scenery. I read, before I made the journey, Hutchings's book, Professor Whitney's book, and all the accounts of the valley I could lay my hands on. Yet, when I came to see the valley, it was as though I had never read a line concerning it. All I had read passed out of my mind in the presence of those stupendous rocks; all I had seen was as nothing compared with the grand, white, scarred granite face of El Capitan, which rears its precipitous side 3300 feet above the level along which you ride.

El Capitan is, to me, altogether the grandest sight in the valley. The Sentinel Dome is 1200 feet higher; the Glacier Rock is nearly as high; and even the Three Brothers—weird, and deserving the picturesque name

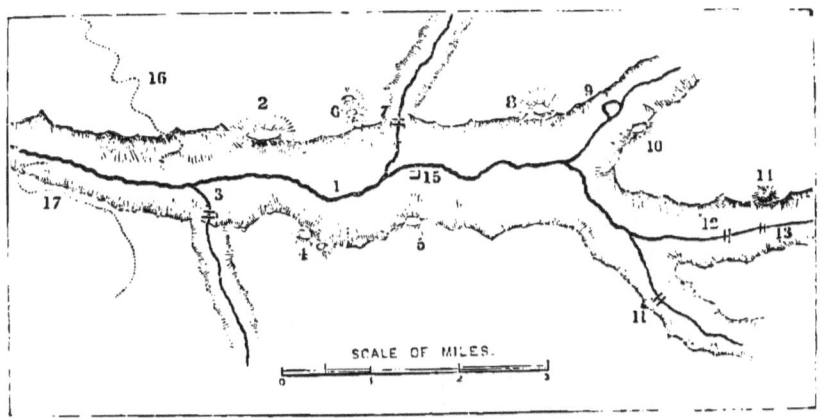

PLAN OF THE YOSEMITE VALLEY.

References.—1. Merced River.—2. El Capitan.—3. Bridal Veil Fall.—4. Cathedral Rocks.—5. Sentinel.—6. Three Brothers.—7. Yosemite Fall.—8. North Dome.—9. Mirror Lake.—10. South Dome.—11. South Fork Fall. —12. Vernal Fall.—13. Nevada Fall.—14. Bellows Butte.—15. Hutchings's Hotel.—16. Coulterville Trail.— 17. Mariposa Trail.

of the "Jumping Frogs," which the Indians gave them—surpass El Capitan in altitude; but none of them approach in impressiveness this stupendous, solid, seamless, cream-white mass of rock, which shines with a subdued polish as though it had been carved out of ivory. It is not a mere rock or summit, but a vast wall, nearly two miles broad, which seems to dominate the valley as you ride in on either trail, and whose grandeur grows upon you with every step your horse takes.

When you have reached your hotel, no doubt some impatient spirits will at once gather around you and attempt to lay out for you to-morrow's and the next day's routine of sight-seeing. Drive them away, and determine in your own mind not to be hurried. After breakfast next day take a book—any book will do, but Whitney's little "Yosemite Guide" is the best for the place—sit down on the hotel veranda, in front of the Great Yosemite Fall, and look at that. It will, if you are anything better than a mere owl, if you have but a spark of love for fine natural scenery, repay you. You will see the wind play many fantastic tricks with the long, glittering, foaming band of water as it pours and roars down from the awful height. And as you sit there you will get, but slowly, as at Niagara also, some true conception into your mind of the grandeur of the scene. By-and-by, after your mid-day meal, you may ride out; and, if you pick your way over to the foot of the Yosemite Fall, you will be rewarded for your adventure by seeing what a body of water it is that tumbles down before your eyes for 2600 feet from the top of the vast precipice.

The guides will not let you miss any of the sights of the valley; and it is curious how quickly the visitor learns to recognize each of the great falls and summits. I do not mean, therefore, to trouble the reader here with a detailed account of these. The illustrations given herewith show all the most noteworthy objects. The one least worth seeing is the Mirror Lake. If you follow the bank of the roaring Merced down, on an afternoon, till you reach El Capitan, you will probably see a sight far finer than Mirror Lake affords, for the Merced has a quiet pool, large enough to reflect El Capitan himself; and it will seem to you the most magnificent shadow your eyes ever beheld.

The finest excursion within the valley is to the Nevada Falls, which requires a whole day, especially if you climb up to the top of this magnificent fall, which any healthy person can do, and which ladies and children are sure to enjoy. You leave the hotel as soon after breakfast as is convenient, dine at Snow's, at the top of the Vernal Fall, at half-past eleven or twelve o'clock (and Mrs. Snow will give you an excellent and abundant dinner); then climb up to the top of the Nevada Fall, or ride up, if the new bridle-path is opened, peep into the singular ravine called the Little Yosemite, wander about on the rocky crags over which the Nevada tumbles, return to Snow's, go down the ladders past the Vernal Fall—a very easy and safe descent—and find your horses waiting for you below for a pleasant canter back to the hotel.

Take with you into the valley, above all books, Whitney's "Yosemite Guide-Book." The author was the State geologist of California. His little work, published by Little, Brown & Co., Boston, will fit your coat-pocket, and will interest you more than any novel; and you will be encouraged by it to do what ladies and children can do with perfect safety and convenience, what everybody ought to do, but few do—make the tour of the *rim* of the valley. A party of four or a dozen can make this journey in four or five days, carrying with them provisions, shelter and covers, on animals, and gaining an enjoyment unique in every way, and views of the valley which cannot in any other manner be obtained.

NEVADA FALL, YOSEMITE VALLEY.

If you have time to visit Mount Shasta, this tour, beginning at Sacramento, will give you a sight of the whole of the great Sacramento Valley. The valley closes in as you journey northward; and at Red Bluff, which is the head of navigation on the river, you have a magnificent view of Lassen's Peaks on the east—twin peaks, snow-clad, and rising high out of the plain—and also of the majestic snow-covered crag which is known as Shasta Butte, which towers high above the mountains to the north, and, though here one hundred and twenty miles off, looks but a day's ride away.

Redding, thirty miles north from Shasta, lies at the head of the Sacramento Valley. From there a line of stage-coaches proceeds north into Oregon, through the mass of mountains which separates the Sacramento

Valley in California from the Willamette Valley in Oregon. The stage-road passes through a very varied and picturesque country, one which few pleasure-travellers see, and which yet is as well worth a visit as any part of the western coast. The Sacramento River, which rises in a large spring near the base of Mount Shasta, has worn its way through the high mountains, and rushes down for nearly a hundred miles of its course an impetuous, roaring mountain stream, abounding in trout at all seasons, and in June, July, and August filled with salmon, which have come up here through the Golden Gates from the ocean to spawn. The stage-road follows almost to its source the devious course of the river, and you ride along sometimes nearly on a level with the stream, and again on a road-bed cut out of the steep mountain-side a thousand or fifteen hundred feet above the river; through fine forests of sugar-pines and yellow pines, many of which come almost up to the dimensions of the great sequoias. The river and its upper tributaries abound in trout, and this region is famous among California sportsmen for deer and fish.

CATHEDRAL ROCKS, YOSEMITE VALLEY.

RUNNING THE ROOKERIES—GATHERING MURRE EGGS.

CHAPTER IV.

THE FARALLON ISLANDS.

IF you should approach the harbor of San Francisco from the sea, your first sight of land would be a collection of picturesque rocks known as the Farallones, or, more fully, the Farallones de los Frayles. They are six rugged islets, whose peaks lift up their heads in picturesque masses out of the ocean, twenty-three and a half miles from the Golden Gate, the famous entrance of San Francisco Bay. Farallon is a Spanish word, meaning a small pointed islet in the sea.

These rocks, probably of volcanic origin, and bare and desolate, lie in a line from south-east to north-west—curiously enough the same line in which the islands of the Hawaiian or Sandwich Islands group have been thrown up. Geologists say they are the outcrop of an immense granite dike.

The southernmost island, which is the largest — just as Hawaii, the southernmost of the Sandwich Islands group, is also the biggest — extends for nearly a mile east and west, and is three hundred and forty feet high. It is composed of broken and water-worn rocks, forming numerous angular peaks, and having several caves; and the rock, mostly barren and bare, has here and there a few weeds and a little grass. At one point there is a small beach, and at another a depression; but the fury of the waves makes landing at all times difficult, and for the most part impossible.

The Farallones are seldom visited by travellers or pleasure-seekers. The wind blows fiercely here most of the time; the ocean is rough; and, to persons subject to sea-sickness, the short voyage is filled with the misery of that affliction. Yet they contain a great deal that is strange and curious. On the highest point of the South Farallon the Government has placed a light-house, a brick tower, seventeen feet high, surmounted by a lantern and illuminating apparatus. It has a revolving white light, showing a prolonged flash of ten seconds' duration once in a minute. The light is about three hundred and sixty feet above the sea, and with a clear atmosphere is visible, from an elevation of ten feet, twenty-five and a half miles distant; from an elevation of sixty feet it can be seen nearly thirty-one miles away; and it is plainly visible from Sulphur Peak, on the mainland, thirty-four hundred and seventy-one feet high, and sixty-four and a half miles distant. The light-house is in latitude $37° 41' 8''$ north, and longitude $122° 59' 05''$ west.

On our foggy Western coast it has been necessary to place the light-houses low, because if they stood too high their light would be hidden in fog-banks and low clouds. The tower on the South Farallon is, therefore, low; and this, no doubt, is an advantage also to the light-keepers, who are less exposed to the buffetings of the storm than if their labor and care lay at a higher elevation.

As the Farallones lie in the track of vessels coming from the westward to San Francisco, the light is one of the most important, as it is also one of the most powerful, on our Western coast; and it is supplemented by a fog-whistle, which is one of the most curious contrivances of this kind in the world. It is a huge trumpet, six inches in diameter at its smaller end, and blown by the rush of air through a cave or passage connecting with the ocean.

One of the numerous caves worn into the rocks by the surf had a hole at the top, through which the incoming breakers violently expelled the air they carried before them. Such spout-holes are not uncommon on rugged, rocky coasts. There are several on the Mendocino coast, and a number on the shores of the Sandwich Islands. This one, however, has been utilized by the ingenuity of man. The mouth-piece of the trumpet or fog-whistle is fixed against the aperture in the rock, and the breaker, dashing in with venomous spite, or the huge, bulging wave which would dash a ship to pieces and drown her crew in a single effort, now blows the fog-whistle and warns the mariner off. The sound thus produced has been heard at a distance of seven or eight miles. It has a peculiar effect, because it has no regular period; depending upon the irregular coming in of the waves, and upon their similarly irregular force, it is blown somewhat as an idle boy would blow his penny trumpet. It ceases entirely for an hour and a half at low-water, when the mouth of the cave or passage is exposed.

The life of the keepers of the Farallon light is singularly lonely and monotonous. Their house is built somewhat under the shelter of the rocks, but they live in what to a landsman would seem a perpetual storm; the ocean roars in their ears day and night; the boom of the surf is their constant and only music; the wild scream of the sea-birds, the howl of the sea-lions, the whistle and shriek of the gale, the dull, threatening thunder of the vast breakers, are the dreary and desolate sounds which lull them to sleep at night, and assail their ears when they awake. In the winter months even their supply-vessel, which, for the most part, is their only connection with the world, is sometimes unable to make a landing for weeks at a time. Chance visitors they see only occasionally, and at the distance at which a steamer is safe from the surf, and at which a girl could not even recognize her lover. The commerce of San Francisco passes before their eyes, but so far away that they cannot tell the ships and steamers which sail by them voiceless and without greeting; and of the events passing on the planet with which they have so frail a social tie they learn only at long and irregular intervals. The change from sunshine to fog is the chief variety in their lives; the hasty landing of supplies the great event in their months. They cannot even watch the growth of trees and plants; and, to a child born and reared in such a place, a sunny lee under the shelter of rocks is probably the ideal of human felicity.

Except the rock of Tristan d'Acunha, in the Southern Atlantic Ocean, I have never seen an inhabited spot which seemed so utterly desolate, so entirely separated from the world, whose people appeared to me to have

LIGHT-HOUSE OF THE SOUTH FARALLON.

such a slender hold on mankind. Yet, for their solace, they know that a powerful Government watches over their welfare, and—if that is any comfort—that, thirty miles away, there are lights and music and laughter and singing, as well as crowds, and all the anxieties and annoyances incidental to what we are pleased to call civilization.

But though these lonely rocks contain but a small society of human beings—the keepers and their families—they are filled with animal life; for they are the home of a multitude of sea-lions, and a vast number of birds and rabbits.

The rabbits, which live on the scanty herbage growing among the rocks, are descended from a few pairs brought here many years ago, when some speculative genius thought to make a huge rabbit-warren of these rocks for the supply of the San Francisco market. These little animals are not very wild. In the dry season they feed on the bulbous roots of the grass, and sometimes they suffer from famine. In the winter and spring they are fat, and then their meat is white and sweet. During summer and fall they are not fit to eat.

They increase very rapidly, and at not infrequent intervals over-populate the island, and then perish by hundreds of starvation and the diseases which follow a too meagre diet. They are of all colors; and though descended from some pairs of white rabbits, seem to have reverted in color to the wild race from which they originated.

The Farallones have no snakes.

The sea-lions, which congregate by thousands upon the cliffs, and bark, and howl, and shriek, and roar in the caves and upon the steep, sunny slopes, are but little disturbed, and one can usually approach them within twenty or thirty yards. It is an extraordinarily interesting sight to see these marine monsters, many of them bigger than an ox, at play in the surf, and to watch the superb skill with which they know how to control their own motions when a huge wave seizes them, and seems likely to dash them to pieces against the rocks. They love to lie in the sun upon the bare and warm rocks; and here they sleep, crowded together, and lying upon each other in inextricable confusion.

The bigger the animal, the greater his ambition appears to be to climb to the highest summit; and when a huge, slimy beast has with infinite squirming attained a solitary peak, he does not tire of raising his sharp-pointed, maggot-like head, and complacently looking about him. They are a rough set of brutes—rank bullies, I should say; for I have watched them repeatedly as a big one shouldered his way among his fellows, reared his huge front to intimidate some lesser seal which had secured a favorite spot, and first with howls, and, if this did not suffice, with teeth and main force, expelled the weaker from his lodgment. The smaller sea-lions, at least those which have left their mothers, appear to have no rights which any one is bound to respect. They get out of the way with an abject promptness which proves that they live in terror of the stronger members of the community; but they do not give up their places without harsh complaints and piteous groans.

Plastered against the rocks, and with their lithe and apparently boneless shapes conformed to the rude and sharp angles, they are a wonderful, but not a graceful or pleasing, sight. At a little distance they look like huge maggots, and their slow, ungainly motions upon the land do not lessen this resemblance. Swimming in the ocean, at a distance from the

SEA-LIONS.

land, they are inconspicuous objects, as nothing but the head shows above water, and that only at intervals. But when the vast surf which breaks in mountain waves against the weather side of the Farallones with a force which would in a single sweep dash to pieces the biggest Indiaman—

when such a surf, vehemently and with apparently irresistible might, lifts its tall, white head, and with a deadly roar lashes the rocks half-way to their summit—then it is a magnificent sight to see a dozen or half a hundred great sea-lions at play in the very midst and fiercest part of the boiling surge, so completely masters of the situation that they allow themselves to be carried within a foot or two of the rocks, and at the last and imminent moment, with an adroit twist of their bodies, avoid the shock, and, diving, re-appear beyond the breaker.

As I sat, fascinated with this weird spectacle of the sea-lions, which seemed to me like an unhallowed prying into some hidden and monstrous secret of nature, I could better realize the fantastic and brutal wildness of life in the earlier geological ages, when monsters and chimeras dire wallowed about our unripe planet, and brute force of muscles and lungs ruled among the populous hordes of beasts which, fortunately for us, have perished, leaving us only this great, wild sea-beast as a faint reminiscence of their existence. I wondered what Dante would have thought, and what new horrors his gloomy imagination would have conjured, could he have watched these thousand or two of sea-lions at their sports.

The small, sloping, pointed head of the creature gives it, to me, a peculiarly horrible appearance. It seems to have no brain, and presents an image of life with the least intelligence. It is in reality not without wits, for one needs only to watch the two or three specimens in the great tank at Woodward's Gardens, when they are getting fed, to see that they instantly recognize their keeper, and understand his voice and motion. But all their wit is applied to the basest uses. Greed for food is their ruling passion, and the monstrous, lightning-like lunges through the water, the inarticulate shrieks of pleasure or of fury, as he dashes after his food or comes up without it, the wild, fierce eyes, the eager and brutal vigor with which he snatches a morsel from a smaller fellow-creature, the reliance on strength alone, and the abject and panic-struck submission of the weaker to the stronger—all this shows him a brute of the lowest character.

Yet there is a wonderful, snake-like grace in the lithe, swift motions of the animal when he is in the surf. You forget the savage, blood-shot eyes, the receding forehead, the clumsy figure and awkward motion, as he wriggles up the steep rocks, the moment you see him at his superb sport in the breakers. It seemed to me that he was another creature. The eye looks less baleful, and even joyous; every movement discloses conscious power; the excitement of the sport sheds from him somewhat of the brutality which re-appears the moment he lands or seeks his food.

So far as I could learn, the Farallon sea-lions are seldom disturbed by men seeking profit from them. In the egging season one or two are shot to supply oil to the lamps of the eggers; and occasionally one is caught for exhibition on the main-land. How do they catch a sea-lion? Well, they lasso him, and, odd as it sounds, it is the best and probably the only way to capture this beast. An adroit Spaniard, to whom the lasso or reata is like a fifth hand, or like the trunk to the elephant, steals up to a sleeping congregation, fastens his eye on the biggest of the lot, and, biding his time, at the first motion of the animal, with unerring skill flings his

SHAGS, MURRES, AND SEA-GULLS.

loose rawhide noose, and then holds on for dear life. It is the weight of an ox and the vigor of half a dozen that he has tugging at the other end of his rope; and if a score of men did not stand ready to help, and it were not possible to take a turn of the reata around a solid rock, the seal would surely get away.

Moreover, they must handle the beast tenderly, for it is easily injured. Its skin, softened by its life in the water, is quickly cut by the rope; its bones are easily broken; and its huge frame, too rudely treated, may be so hurt that the life dies out of it. As quickly as possible the captured sea-lion is stuffed into a strong box or cage, and here, in a cell too narrow to permit movement, it roars and yelps in helpless fury until it is transported to its tank. Wild and fierce as it is, it seems to reconcile itself to the tank life very rapidly. If the narrow space of its big bath-tub frets it, you do not perceive this, for hunger is its chief passion, and with a moderately full stomach the animal does well in captivity—of course with sufficient water.

The South Farallon is the only inhabited one of the group. The remainder are smaller—mere rocky points sticking up out of the Pacific. The Middle Farallon is a single rock, from fifty to sixty yards in diameter, and twenty or thirty feet above the water. It lies two and a half miles north-west by west from the light-house. The North Farallon consists, in fact, of four pyramidal rocks, whose highest peak, in the centre of the group, is one hundred and sixty feet high; the southern rock of the four is twenty feet high. The four have a diameter of one hundred and sixty, one hundred and eighty-five, one hundred and twenty-five, and thirty-five yards respectively, and the most northern of the islets bears north 64° west from the Farallon light, six and three-fifths miles distant.

All the islands are frequented by birds; but the largest, the South Farallon, on which the light-house stands, is the favorite resort of these creatures, who come here in astonishing numbers every summer to breed; and it is to this island that the eggers resort at that season to obtain supplies of sea-birds' eggs for the San Francisco market, where they have a regular and large sale.

The birds which breed upon the Farallones are gulls, murres, shags, and sea-parrots, the last a kind of penguin. The eggs of the shags and parrots are not used, but the eggers destroy them, to make more room for the other birds. The gull begins to lay about the middle of May, and usually ten days before the murre. The gull makes a rude nest of brush

THE GULL'S NEST.

and sea-weed upon the rocks; the murre does not take even this much trouble, but lays its eggs in any convenient place on the bare rocks.

The gull is soon through, but the murre continues to lay for about two

average of twenty-six cents per dozen. There has been, I was assured by the manager, no sensible decrease in the number of the birds or the eggs during twenty years.

From fifteen to twenty men are employed during the egging season in collecting and shipping the eggs. They live on the island during that time in rude shanties near the usual landing-place. The work is not amusing, for the birds seek out the least accessible places, and the men must follow, often climbing where a goat would almost hesitate. But this is not the worst. The gull sits on her nest, and resists the robber who comes for her eggs, and he must take care not to get bitten. The murre remains until her enemy is close upon her; then she rises with a scream which often startles a thousand or two of birds, who whirl up into the air in a dense mass, scattering filth and guano over the eggers.

Nor is this all. The gulls, whose season of breeding is soon past, are extravagantly fond of murre eggs; and these rapacious birds follow the egg-gatherers, hover over their heads, and no sooner is a murre's nest uncovered than the bird swoops down, and the egger must be extremely quick, or the gull will snatch the prize from under his nose. So greedy and eager are the gulls that they sometimes even wound the eggers, striking them with their beaks. But if the gull gets an egg he flies up with it, and, tossing it in the air, swallows what he can catch, letting the shell and half its contents fall in a shower upon the luckless and disappointed egger below.

Finally, so difficult is the ground that it is impossible to carry baskets. The egger therefore stuffs the eggs into his shirt-bosom until he has as many as he can safely carry, then clambers over rocks and down precipices until he comes to a place of deposit, where he puts them into baskets, to be carried down to the shore, where there are houses for receiving them. But so skilful and careful are the gatherers that but few eggs are broken.

The gathering proceeds daily, when it has once begun, and the whole ground is cleared off, so that no stale eggs shall remain. Thus if a portion of the ground has been neglected for a day or two, all the eggs must be flung into the sea, so as to begin afresh. As the season advances the operations are somewhat contracted, leaving a part of the island undisturbed for breeding; and the gathering of eggs is stopped entirely about a month before the birds usually leave the island, so as to give them all an opportunity to hatch out a brood.

The murre is not eatable. If undisturbed, it lays two eggs only; when robbed, it will keep on laying until it has produced six or even

A CONTEST FOR THE EGGS.

eight eggs; and the manager of the islands told me that he had found as many as eight eggs forming in a bird's ovaries when killed and opened in the beginning of the season. The male bird regularly relieves the female on the nest, and also watches to resist the attacks of the gull, which not only destroys the eggs but also eats the young. The murre feeds on sea-grass and jelly-fish, and I was assured that though some hundreds had been examined at different times, no fish had ever been found in a murre's stomach.

The bird is small, about the size of a half-grown duck, but its egg is as large as a goose-egg. The egg is brown or greenish, and speckled.

When quite fresh it has no fishy taste, but when two or three days old the fishy taste becomes perceptible. They are largely used in San Francisco by the restaurants and bakers, for omelets, cakes, and custards.

During the height of the egging season the gulls hover in clouds over the rocks, and when a rookery is started, and the poor birds leave their nests by hundreds, the air is presently alive with gulls flying off with the eggs, and the eggers are sometimes literally drenched.

THE GREAT ROOKERY.

There is thus inevitably a considerable waste of eggs. I asked some of the eggers how many murres nested on the South Farallon, and they thought at least one hundred thousand. I do not suppose this an extravagant estimate, for, taking the season of 1872, when seventeen thousand nine hundred and fifty-two dozen eggs were actually sold in San Francisco, and allowing half a dozen to each murre, this would give nearly thirty-six thousand birds; and adding the proper number for eggs broken, destroyed by gulls, and not gathered, the number of murres and gulls is probably over one hundred thousand: this on an island less than a mile in its greatest diameter, and partly occupied by the light-house and fog-whistle and their keepers, and by other birds and a large number of sea-lions.

When they are done laying, and when the young can fly, the birds leave the island, usually going off together. During the summer and fall they return in clouds at intervals, but stay only a few days at a time, though there are generally a few to be found at all times; and I am told that eggs in small quantities can be found in the fall.

The murre does not fly high, nor is it a very active bird, or apparently of long flight. But the eggers say that when it leaves the island they do not know whither it goes, and they assert that it is not abundant on the neighboring coast. The young begin to fly when they are two weeks old, and the parents usually take them immediately into the water.

The sea-parrot has a crest, and somewhat resembles a cockatoo. Its numbers on the South Farallon are not great. It makes a nest in a hole in the rocks, and bites if it is disturbed. The island was first used as a sealing station; but this was not remunerative, there being but very few fur seal, and no sea-otters. This animal, which abounds in Alaska, and is found occasionally on the southern coast of California, frequents the masses of kelp which line the shore; but there is no kelp about the Farallones.

In the early times of California, when provisions were high-priced, the egg-gatherers sometimes got great gains. Once, in 1853, a boat absent but three days brought in one thousand dozen, and sold the whole cargo at a dollar a dozen; and in one season thirty thousand dozen were gathered, and brought an average of but little less than this price.

Of course there was an egg war. The prize was too great not to be struggled for; and the rage of the conflicting claimants grew to such a pitch that guns were used and lives were threatened, and at last the Government of the United States had to interfere to keep the peace. But with lower prices the strife ceased: the present company bought out, I believe, all adverse claims, and for the last fifteen or sixteen years peace has reigned in this part of the county of San Francisco—for these lonely islets are a part of the same county with the metropolis of the Pacific.

SNOW-PLOUGH ON THE CENTRAL PACIFIC RAILROAD.

CHAPTER V.

SOUTHERN CALIFORNIA FOR INVALIDS.

A FRIEND and neighbor of my own, consumptive for some years, and struggling for his life in a winter residence for two years at Nice and Mentone, and during a third at Aiken, in South Carolina, came, one October, to Southern California.

He had been "losing ground," as he said, and, as his appearance showed, for two years, and the previous summer, suffered so severely from night-sweats, sleeplessness, continual coughing, and lack of appetite, that it was doubtful whether he would live through the winter anywhere; and it was rather in desperation, than with much hope of a prolonged or comfortable life, that he made ready for the journey across the continent, with his family.

In January following I was one day standing in the door-way of a hotel at Los Angeles, when I saw a wagon drive up; the driver jumped out, held out his hand to me, and sung out, in a hearty voice, "How do you do?" It was my consumptive friend—but a changed man.

He had just driven sixty miles in two days, over a rough road, from San Bernardino—there was no railroad in Southern California in those days. He walked with me several miles on the evening we met; he ate heartily and slept well, enjoyed his life, and coughed hardly at all. It was an amazing change to come about in three months, and in a man so ill as he had been.

"I shall never be a sound man, of course," he said to me, when I spent some days with him, later, at San Bernardino; "but this climate has added some years to my life; it has given me ease and comfort; and neither Nice, nor Mentone, nor Aiken are, in my opinion, to be compared with some parts of Southern California in point of climate for consumptives."

This was nearly ten years ago, and in those days there were few conveniences and no comforts for invalids in Southern California. The climate, which enables consumptives to live out-of-doors almost the whole time, was pretty much the only advantage which offered itself in those days; and the poorly cooked food, the rough roads, the scanty accommodations, and, above all, the lack of knowledge of what spots are most favorable to certain forms of disease—all these made the search for health, or for comfortable and enjoyable existence, at that time, a matter of some difficulty.

Since then all this has changed. Hotel accommodations, at all the resorts for invalids, have greatly improved; and new points have been discovered by the care of competent and skilful physicians, and the experience of numbers of persons in weak health, especially consumptives; so that the seeker after health has now the opportunity to try a much larger variety of climate, and to get comfortable and even luxurious accommodations in places where, ten years ago, he had to put up with hard fare and lodgings. Moreover, the extension of the Southern Pacific Railroad system has brought the best health resorts within easy reach of invalids; and where a day's drive is necessary, that is an advantage rather than otherwise, because the seeker after health will get more of what he wants in the sunshine and open air than in houses or cars.

There is no longer any doubt of the very great and often surprising beneficial influences upon diseases of the throat and lungs, of the dry and warm winter climate of Southern California. One may meet in every county of this part of the State people who, having tender throats or lungs, came thither from the East or Europe, and have made a complete recovery. I know myself, not dozens but hundreds of instances, of men and women who would have perished in the more Eastern part of the United States, though for the greater part these were not what are called "confirmed invalids"—they were men and women to whom our Eastern winters are seasons of discomfort and dread, of "staying in the house," coughing, depressed spirits, and doctor's bills—who, after a winter in California, found themselves capable of enduring fatigue and exposure with enjoyment, and who had lost that uncomfortable consciousness of "having a throat," which is so often the bane of life among us. That the climate, with proper care in living, will eradicate the tendency toward

SUMMIT OF THE SIERRAS, FROM CENTRAL PACIFIC RAILROAD.

consumption and throat and lung troubles, there is now a very large amount of evidence to prove; as also that it will insure to the actual consumptive—to a person already stricken with this disease—a much larger remainder of comfortable life, and of enjoyment, than is attainable elsewhere in this country.

Experience has shown that it is not prudent for invalids or health-seekers to settle directly near the sea-shore anywhere in California.

The sea-air, there as here, is not auspicious to those with weak lungs or throats. But it is surprising how slight a removal from the sea makes all the change needed. At Santa Barbara, formerly, a friend of my own, loving the sea, chose to spend the winter quite near the shore. She enjoyed her life, but she did not gain strength as rapidly as she hoped and had been led to expect, until one of the most experienced physicians of the place quietly advised her to remove to a little distance from the beach. She removed to a house less than a mile away, and felt the benefit of this slight change from the very first day. It was because of several such experiences as these that the Arlington Hotel, at Santa Barbara, one of the best and most comfortable in all Southern California, was built at a proper distance from the shore; and it is, I think, as much owing to the advantage of its situation, protected from the sea-air by the *mesa*, and having a peculiarily dry as well as pure air, as to the comfort and tasteful elegance of its arrangements and surroundings, that it has been for some years, and remains, a favorite resort for Eastern invalids. It combines, in greater perfection than any other hotel in Southern California, all the details which are needed to make the life of an invalid or healthseeker pleasant and cheerful—sunny rooms, open fires, broad and roomy piazzas, closed in with glass at that part exposed to the prevailing breezes; spacious and well-kept grounds, with green lawns, and abundant flowers all the winter as well as the summer through; roomy parlors, well warmed by wood fires; and a good table. I speak of it in this detail because it is still too often the case in Southern California that the health resort presents few attractions to the invalid, except the climate; and it is now so easy to maintain a green and smooth lawn, to build sheltered and roomy piazzas, and to provide sunshiny rooms and open fires, that invalids have a right to demand these comforts. Of course, in business places like Los Angeles and San Diego, these special conveniences and attractions are not expected; the health-seeker must take his chance with the rest of the world while he is staying there. San Diego has still its charming, sunshiny climate, but less has been done there than in some other places in the southern part of the State to invite and render pleasant the invalid's stay. In fact, the pleasant, quaint town changed but little in the last ten years, until the long-delayed arrival of a railroad has given it the bustling life of a seaport.

Santa Barbara, more than all the health-resorts of ten years ago, has gained in real advantages to the invalid. It has, as I have said, the best arranged and most pleasantly placed hotel in the southern half of the State, and has, besides, natural and acquired advantages which give it a peculiar charm. The nearness of the mountains to the sea-shore here gives it an undoubted climatic advantage, as the foot-hills here come down almost to the sea; and it is in the foot-hills, everywhere in the State, as experience has shown, that the finest climate is found. At Santa Barbara mountain and sea combine to make a singularly charming landscape; and the numerous little valleys in the foot-hills, flower-covered and wonderfully lovely in winter and spring, tempt the sojourner and health-seeker to daily excursions on horseback, always safe, and yet having the

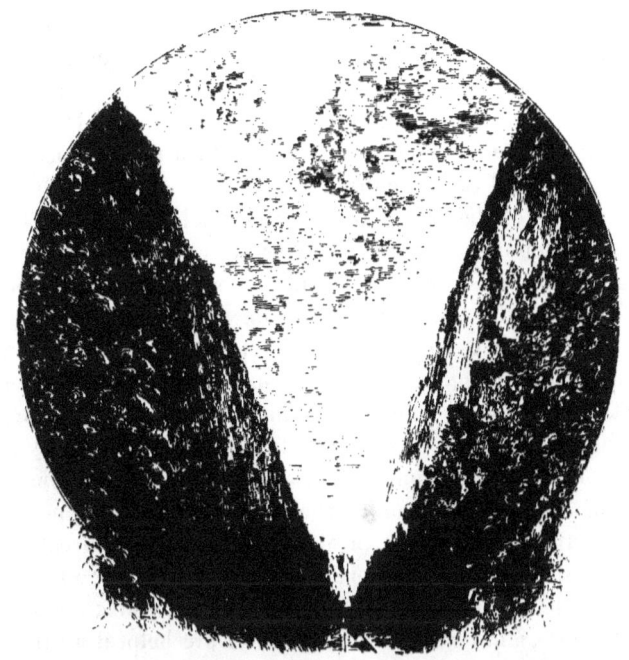

BLOOMER CUT, CENTRAL PACIFIC RAILROAD.

charm and excitement of exploration and discovery. Thus there is hereabouts very much to engage the mind of a health-seeker—amusement and excitement of kinds which in themselves are health-promoting, as well as sure to carry off dolorous thoughts of self.

Aside from these excursions for a day or an afternoon, the neighborhood affords a variety of longer drives: up the coast to the Gaviota Pass, or down the coast to the Carpenteria and Ventura; and if the health-seeker desires an entire change of air and scene, such as sometimes proves so beneficial to invalids, he has it ready to his hand in one of the pleasantest day's drives he can find anywhere in the State—to the Ojai Valley, where he can spend a week or a month at his pleasure with comfort and benefit. The Ojai Valley (pronounced Ohy) is reached by a drive of thirty-eight miles by way of the Carpenteria and the Cassitas Pass. It is a plain of about fifteen miles by three or four, surrounded by picturesque mountains of from two to three thousand feet high. The valley is famous even in California for the abundance and loveliness of its woods of evergreen oaks. It presents the appearance, in fact, of a magnificent old English park; the oaks dot the surface of the whole lower valley, and are scattered over it in single specimens and clumps—the perfection of what in England is called the "natural" style in landscape gardening. There is no underbrush or small growth; and one wanders at will under noble trees, or rides or drives for miles through a piece of natural scenery which combines the utmost loveliness of nature with a finish which gives the impression of art and careful culture.

In the middle of the Ojai Valley lies a little hamlet, which the people have been kind enough to name after the author of this book. Beneath the shade of fine oaks, and in the midst of what has the air of a great park, are two cheerful and comfortable inns, the Ojai Valley House and the Oak Glen Cottage, both admirably kept, which have acquired a deserved popularity among health-seekers and travellers in Southern California. The Ojai Valley offers many interesting excursions, drives, and rides, to the sojourner at these pretty little inns; and the dry and pure air of the valley has been found especially favorable to persons to whom even that of Santa Barbara, or of the Sierra Madre Villa, near Los Angeles, is too strong—persons with abnormally sensitive throats or lungs. It is a lovely, sheltered nook, where the frailest invalids are benefited, and where neither sea-fog nor a too bracing air can penetrate; and its scenery, varied but gentle, and its soft, warm sunshine are helpful all through the year, but especially in winter, to the invalid. Both at Santa Barbara and in the Ojai Valley strangers find the advantages of a pleasant, cultivated society, with churches, schools, and the moral and intellectual atmosphere of a New England community; and this is no small benefit to strangers seeking health away from home.

Half an hour by rail from Los Angeles, and about two miles distant from the old mission of San Gabriel, perched high at the base of the mountains, lies another well-known winter resort for invalids—the Sierra Madre Villa. This also is a cheerful house, surrounded by orange and lemon groves, and with a distant view of Los Angeles and the ocean. Here, also, the air is dry and the sun warm the winter through; and the

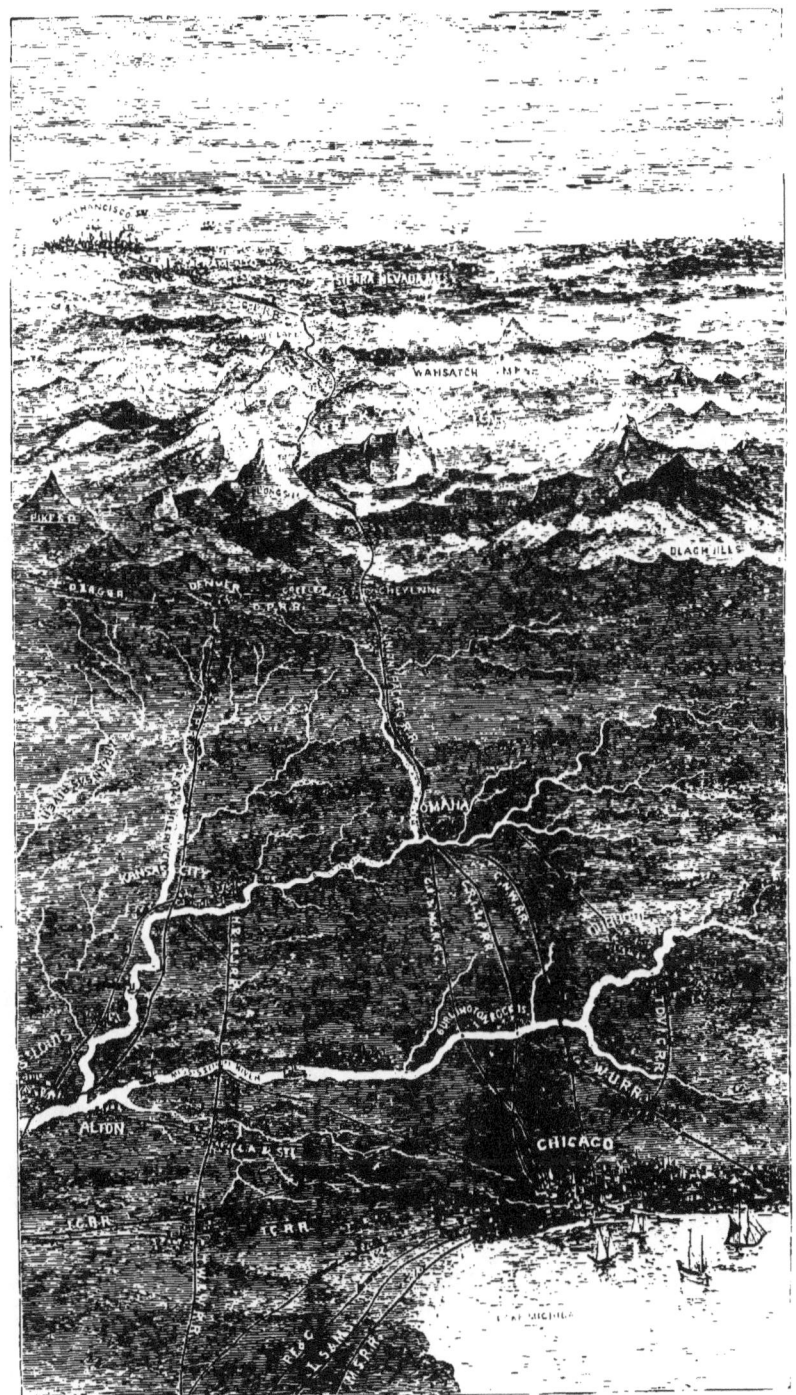

A BIRD'S-EYE VIEW OF THE TRANSCONTINENTAL ROUTE.

surrounding country, largely planted with oranges and other citrous fruits, and vines, with the neighborhood of the largest and most rapidly growing city in the southern part of the State, offer variety to the life of the traveller and invalid.

Riverside, seven miles from San Bernardino, has a pleasant little inn, the Glenwood Cottage, also frequented by invalids, because the air of this whole region included between Riverside, San Bernardino, and the San Gorgonio Pass, is found especially kind to some of the many various forms of lung and throat disease. Riverside also offers the advantage of a cultivated and now uncommonly prosperous community; it is a settlement of intelligent people, largely from New England and the Middle States, who have engaged in the culture of oranges, lemons, and raisins, and have made this so successful that the name of their town is famous throughout California.

At Monterey, only two hours south of San Francisco by rail, there has been built one of the largest and most costly hotels in the State; and this has, on account of the sheltered and warm climate of Monterey, and also because of the comfort and elegance of the hotel and its surroundings, become a famous and very fashionable watering-place, which should be seen by travellers who go to San Francisco.

There are dozens, or even hundreds, of spots throughout Southern California, especially among the foot-hills of the Sierra in the middle part of the San Joaquin Valley, and also about Los Angeles in the foot-hills of the Coast Range, very suitable, so far as climate goes, for the residence of invalids; but they have no comfortable appliances of living, such as health-seekers require to get the full benefit of absence from home. To men and women who are not actually debilitated by disease, but are rather seeking to eradicate dangerous tendencies to throat or lung troubles, or to recover health enfeebled by too persistent application to business or professional duties, the whole of Southern California offers itself as a charmed and charming land. The winter temperature is such as invites to constant out-of-door exercise; and it is quite possible, and very delightful, for a party of friends to buy or hire a wagon and team of horses, with two or three riding-horses—which are still cheaply bought—and, with a competent driver to act as guide and cook, undertake an independent exploration of this southern country. The roads are good; farm or ranch houses are met with at proper intervals, where travellers, if they bring their blankets and some supplies of food, can pass the night comfortably; and the man or woman who has made such a journey from San Diego by San Luis Rey, Anaheim, and Los Angeles to Santa Barbara, will have suf-

THE YOSEMITE VALLEY.

fered no serious hardships, and will have gained a large store of interesting adventure and reminiscence. The whole country is safer than New England for the traveller, who will find only civil treatment and fair dealing everywhere.

Persons who come to California for the winter should bring with them their winter clothing. You do not need a shawl or overcoat if you are exercising, but in driving they are necessary. You can sit out-of-doors almost every day, either to read or write, or in any other occupation; for there are but few rainy days, and it no sooner stops raining than the sun shines out most brilliantly and kindly. I do not think there were five days, either in Santa Barbara or San Diego, in December, January, and February of a winter I passed there, in which the tenderest invalid could not spend the greater part of the day out-of-doors with pleasure and benefit. In Santa Barbara there were not a dozen days during the whole winter in which a baby I know of did not play on the sea-beach. But in the evening you will sit by a wood-fire—mostly with the doors and windows open—and at night you sleep under several blankets very comfortably.

The constant or almost uninterrupted brightness of the skies has, of course, a good deal to do with the healthful influence of the climate.

The southern counties have but little rain. There are no gloomy days. Occasionally there is a fog in the morning, but it is not a cold fog—rather dry and warm, like the Newport fogs.

Moreover, all winter the gardens are full of flowers, the grass is green, and Nature is in her most inviting garb.

The cost of living at hotels and inns is very reasonable. Make them give you a sunny room; for the sun is the source of health and endless comfort in Southern California in winter, and not much less so in summer; and do not hesitate to secure an open wood-fire, for which there is in many places a small extra charge. Horses are cheap and good, and it is an important help to invalids that the air of California makes exercise pleasant and easy, and that the climate of the southern part of the State invites to a free, out-door life at all seasons. I have known weakly women, not accustomed to horseback exercise, to ride, after a few weeks' practice, from five to ten miles in a day, and feel no soreness of the limbs or other unpleasant consequences; and most visitors to California are surprised to find how active a life they can lead, not only without inconvenience but with pleasure and benefit.

At Santa Barbara there is a fine beach, on which the Spanish Californians used in the old times to race their horses. It is as pleasant a stretch of three miles, for a lively canter on horseback, as you can wish for; and there are not five days in the whole winter when you may not take an exhilarating ride there, with the ocean and the islands on one side and the mountains on the other.

At San Diego you have the bay before you, with the Coronados Islands in the blue distance. If you are fond of sailing or fishing, boats are cheaply hired, with competent men to manage them. The shore in some parts affords shells, chiefly a beautiful univalve—the *Abelona*, known to us in the East, commonly, as the "California Shell." If you prefer the shore to the sea, the Julian Mines, about forty miles distant, invite you to a novel excursion, in which you will see some fine farming lands and also fine mountains; and at or near the mines you will find the mountain air exhilarating enough to persuade you, in the spring months, to make a prolonged stay.

Wherever you go, you need to take with you a cheerful and also an inquiring spirit. The whole of Southern California is full of novelties and wonders to an intelligent person; but oftenest he must discover them for himself. From January onward to June you will, if you have eyes for them, discover in your rambles a succession of beautiful, and to you new, wild-flowers. For all healthful, open-air enjoyments you will have extraordinary facilities, because the life is free and untrammelled. You are expected to do what you please; horses are cheap; roads are almost invariably excellent; every place has a good livery-stable; you can get competent guides; and you carry with you, wherever you go, fine mountain scenery, bright sunshine—so constant that, when I remarked to a citizen of San Diego that it was a fine day, he looked at me in amazement, and said, after a pause, "Of course it is a fine day; why not? Every day is fine here." Moreover, at all these places you will meet pleasant, intelligent, and hospitable people, who will add to your enjoyment.

Finally, if you need them, you will find competent physicians; and I advise every invalid who settles for the winter in any one of the places I have mentioned to call in at the beginning that physician of good repute who is longest resident in the place, and get his advice as to clothing, exercise, and what precautions ought to be used in his or her special case. Experience will show you, if the doctor does not at once tell you, whether you can bear close vicinity to the ocean, or whether you will do better two or three miles away from it, on higher ground and nearer the mountains; or farther away still, in some interior valley as the Ojai, mentioned above. In some cases I have known the sea-beach seemed to be the best restorative; in others, close neighborhood to the ocean proved unwholesome, but a change of not more than a mile or two inland worked a speedy, indeed, an almost instant, improvement. The peculiarities of constitution which lead to these differences are not always known beforehand, and only come out with trial and experience.

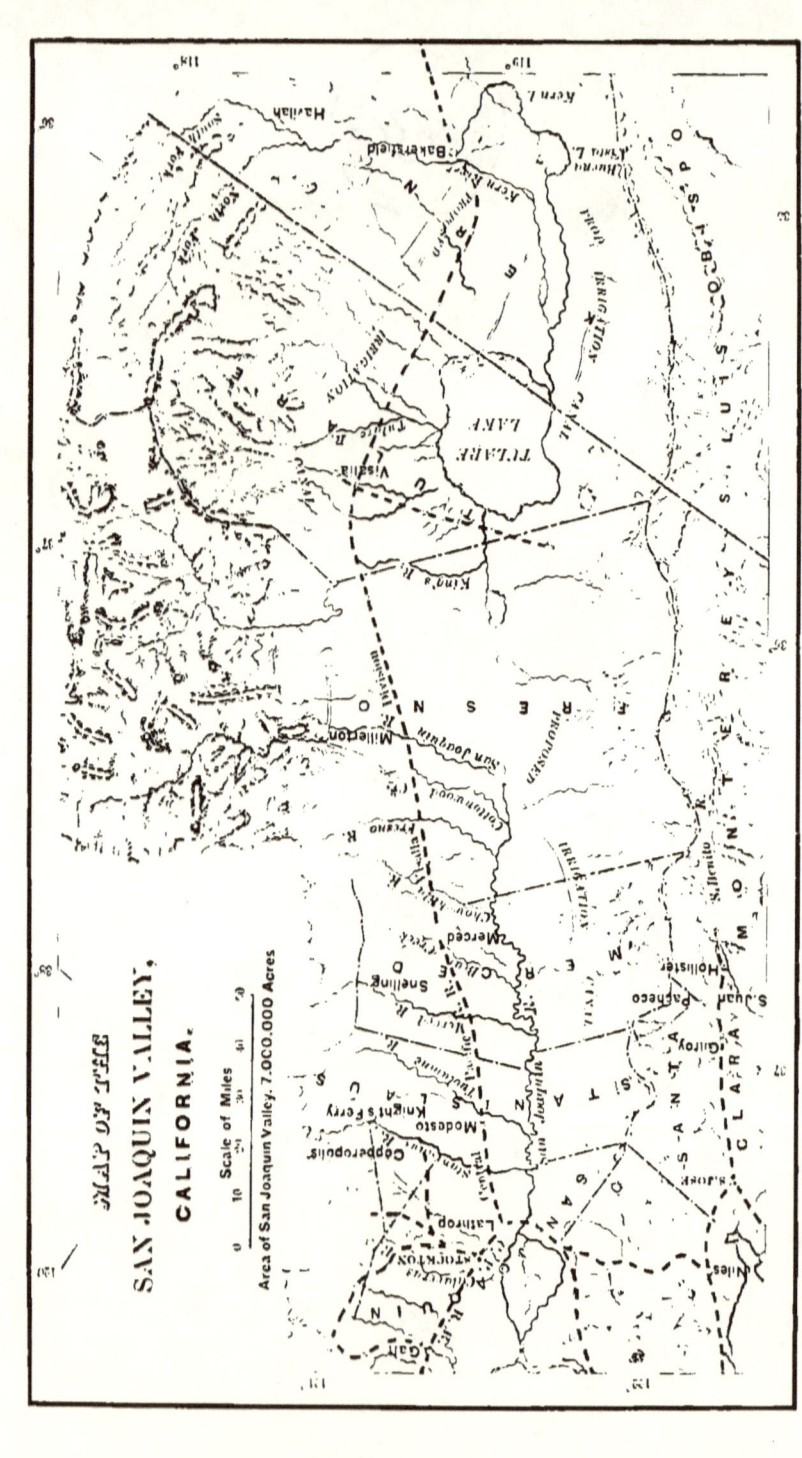

EL CAPITAN.

CHAPTER VI.

THE AGRICULTURAL WEALTH OF CALIFORNIA.—THE GREAT VALLEYS.

THE State of California extends over somewhat more than ten degrees of latitude. If it lay along the Atlantic as it lies along the Pacific coast, its boundaries would include the whole shore-line from Cape Cod to Hilton Head, in South Carolina, and its limits would take in the greater portion of ten of the original States.

It contains two great mountain ranges—the Sierra Nevada and the Coast Range. These, running parallel through the State, approach each other so closely at the south as to leave only the narrow Tejon Pass between them; while at the north they also come together, Mount Shasta rearing its splendid snow-covered summit over the two mountain chains where they are joined.

Enclosed within these mountain ranges lies a long, broad, fertile valley, which was once, no doubt, a great inland sea. It still contains in the southern part three considerable lakes — the Tulare, Kern, and Buena Vista — and is now drained from the south by the San Joaquin River, flowing northward out of these lakes, and from the north by the Sacramento, which rises near the base of Mount Shasta. These two rivers, the one flowing north, the other south, join a few miles below Sacramento, and empty their waters into the bay of San Francisco.

That part of the great inland plain of California which is drained by the Sacramento is called after its river. The Sacramento Valley is forty miles wide, bounded on the west by the Coast Range, and on the east by the Sierra Nevada. It is an immense fertile plain, containing about five millions of acres, becoming mountainous in its northern part, but having a vast area of fertile land, much of which never needs irrigation, and produces fine crops in the driest years. In the spring of 1871, when a drought prevailed nearly all over California, I saw a field of oats of one thousand acres at Chico, on the California and Oregon Railroad, so high that I could and did tie the oats over my head.

The Sacramento Valley has an average rain-fall of about twenty inches, and eighteen inches insure a full crop on soil properly prepared. In 1873 they had less, yet the crops did well wherever the farmers had summer-fallowed the land. This practice is now very general, and is necessary, in order that the grain may have the advantage of the early rains. When a farmer ploughs and prepares his land in the spring or early summer, lets it lie all summer and fall, and sows his grain in November, just as the earliest rain begins, he need not fear for his crop.

There is less difference in climate than one would suppose between the Sacramento and the San Joaquin valleys. Cattle and sheep live out-of-doors, and support themselves all the year round in the Shasta Valley on the north as constantly as in Los Angeles, or any other of the southern counties. The seasons are a little later north than south, but the difference is slight; and as far north as Red Bluff, in the interior, they begin their harvest earlier than in Monterey County, far south, but on the coast. Snow rarely lies on the ground in the northern counties more than a day. The finest varieties of the foreign grapes are hardy everywhere. Light frosts come in December; and in the flower-gardens the geranium withers to the ground, but springs up from the roots again in March. As far north as Redding, at the head of the valley, the mercury very rarely falls below twenty-five degrees, and remains there but a few hours.

As you travel from Marysville, either northward or southward, you will see before and around you a great, wide plain, bounded on the west by the blue outlines of the Coast Range, and on the east by the foot-hills of the Sierra: a great level, over which as far as your eye can reach are scattered groves of grand and picturesque white oaks, which relieve the solitude of the plain, and make it resemble in many parts a well-planted park. Wherever the valley is settled, you will see neat board fences, roomy barns, and farm-houses nestling among trees, and flanked by young orchards. You will not find a great variety of crops, for wheat and barley are the staple products of this valley; and though the farms here are in general of 640 acres or less, there are not wanting some of those immense estates for which California is famous; and a single farmer in this valley is said to have raised on his own land one-twentieth of the entire wheat crop of the State.

Along the banks of the Sacramento there are large quantities of land which is annually overflowed by the river, and much of which is still only used for pasturage during the dry season, when its grasses support large herds of cattle and sheep, which are driven to the uplands when the rains begin to fall. But much of this swamp and tule land has been drained and diked, and is now used for farm land. It produces heavy crops of wheat, and its reclamation has been, and continues to be, one of the successful speculations in land in this State. It will not be long before the shores of the Sacramento and its tributaries will be for many miles so diked that these rivers will never break their bounds, and thus a very considerable area will be added to the fertile farming lands of the State.

It is more thickly inhabited than the southern or San Joaquin Valley, partly because the foot-hills on its eastern side were the scene of the earliest and longest continued, as well as the most successful, mining operations; partly because the Sacramento River is navigable for a longer distance than the San Joaquin, and thus gave facilities for transportation which the lower valley had not; and, finally, because the Sacramento Valley had a railroad completed through its whole extent some years earlier than the San Joaquin Valley.

While the climate of the Sacramento Valley does not differ greatly from that of the San Joaquin, there are yet some important distinctions. Lying farther north, it has more rain: in the upper part of the valley they sometimes see snow; there is not the same necessity for irrigation as in the lower valley; and though oranges flourish in sheltered spots about

Marysville and in Sonoma, and though the almond does well as far north as Chico, yet the cherry, the plum, the peach and the prune, the apricot and nectarine, take the place of the orange, olive, and lemon; and men build their houses somewhat more solidly than farther south.

The romance of the early gold discovery lies mostly in the Sacramento Valley and the adjacent foot-hills. Between Sacramento and Marysville lay Sutter's old fort, and near Marysville is Sutter's farm, where you may still see his groves of fig-trees, under whose shade the country people now hold their picnics; his orchards, which still bear fruit; and his house, which is now a country tavern.

At Stockton begins the great San Joaquin Valley, which has an area of about seven millions of acres. This stretches from Stockton to the Tejon Pass, a length, north and south, of three hundred miles. It has, without including the foot-hills, an average width of forty miles, or with the foot-hills, which contain excellent land, fifty miles. With the foothills on each side, and the smaller mountain valleys, this region has over eighteen million acres of land, of which not less than ten millions are susceptible of highly profitable cultivation. The plains alone contain nearly seven million acres of land.

THE BIG TREES.

The great valley of California, extending from Redding on the north to the Tejon Pass in the south, has a length of four hundred and ten miles, and an area, excluding the foot-hills on each side, of over sixteen thousand square miles. By far the greater part of this great plain consists of alluvial soil, which has washed down from the two mountain ranges which bound it, and it is undoubtedly much the richest large body of land in the United States. Ten years ago it was still, through almost the whole of its extent, used for grazing. Here and there, especially in some parts of the Sacramento Valley, agriculture had made inroads; but in the San Joaquin Valley the "cattle kings" disputed all the ground vigorously with a few humble farmers; and fifteen years ago it was a commonly received doctrine that the San Joaquin plain was unfit for agriculture, because, it was said, the rains were too uncertain, and farming must be mere gambling. In the past ten years, however, a vast change has come about; and agriculture has formally taken possession of the valley.

FLUME AND RAILROAD AT GOLD RUN, SIXTY-FOUR MILES FROM SACRAMENTO.

To an intelligent and observant traveller who has time, no part of the United States, and I am almost tempted to say no part of the world, offers so interesting and instructive a spectacle as he may find in these great valleys of California at this time. It is the spectacle of brains applied to farming in the best manner, and, at the same time, in ways so novel as cannot but delight the observer.

Irrigation is turning the Sacramento and San Joaquin valleys into a vast garden; and here has begun the first experiment in irrigation on a great scale which the Anglo-Saxon race has undertaken. It is already a great and remarkable success; and our American farmers, who have had to adapt themselves in so many curious ways to the exceptional seasons and climate of California, have now proved beyond peradventure that they, better than Hindoos, or Portuguese, or Chinese, or Spaniards, or Italians, can lead down the streams on hitherto sterile plains, and manage water intelligently and effectively, and, what is more, very profitably.

When the first edition of this book was issued, in 1871, there were two or three irrigating ditches in Los Angeles County, one in the San Joaquin Valley, the Farmers' Ditch near Visalia, and none of any extent or importance elsewhere in the State. There was much talk of building canals and tanks on a great and costly scale; but it was still doubted whether farmers—Americans and English-speaking men—would adapt themselves to this novel species of culture. Returning to California after ten years, I am amazed to find many thousands of acres of land under irrigation, planted to orchards, or vines, or growing alfalfa and grain, which land formerly was thought sterile and worthless. I find not hundreds but thousands of pleasant homesteads where before was absolute desert. I find that in these ten years whole colonies or settlements of English-speaking people have not only been collected, but have become permanently prosperous and independent, and many of them wealthy, by the judicious practice of irrigation. I find now miles of valuable orchards where ten years ago cattle were roaming, and cultivated fields where before were only sheep picking up a scanty living for a few months of the year; and I find that the question whether our race can practise irrigation of land, and do it well and profitably, is settled beyond a peradventure.

Not only this, but another equally important question is settled—there is water enough for all uses; and that which seemed to me ten years ago so desirable, and yet so far off, is as good as done—the whole great valley system of California, with its healthful climate and its wonderfully fertile soil, is open to the profitable and happy settlement of a farming population, so far as the overcoming of natural obstacles goes.

A few general and incomplete figures will show on how great a scale lands are now irrigated in California. In Los Angeles and San Bernardino counties, in 1879, 64,490 acres were thus cultivated, with the help of water artificially and systematically applied. In Kern County, 39,940 acres were under irrigation in the same year; in other parts of the San Joaquin Valley, 91,420 acres; in Yolo County, about 10,000 acres. I have not been able to get at complete figures for the whole State, but these accounts will show on how great a scale irrigation has come to be practised within the last ten years. In subsequent chapters I shall endeavor to show Eastern and European farmers and capitalists how profitable and of what easy application this novel feature of agriculture is in the climate of California. It is evident that irrigation is still only in its infancy here. In Kern County, for instance, less than 40,000 acres were irrigated in 1879; but 475,000 acres are, according to official surveys, "susceptible of profitable culture by irrigation"—lie, that is to say, so favorably that water can be laid upon them.

What seems to me of great interest in relation to the present system of irrigation is that, in a large number of cases, the canals, or ditches, are the work of associations of farmers, who have brought down the water for their joint use, and continue to control it, dividing it among themselves, and maintaining their works by an admirable system of co-operation, which in itself shows and must breed intelligence of a high order. In other cases, capitalists have stepped in to build canals and sell the water; but I noticed in the official reports that, in some instances at least, these enterprises, costing great sums of money, have not been profitable, while I heard of no instance in which the same work, accomplished by the co-operation of a body of farmers, has failed of the most satisfactory results. This seems to me as important as it is interesting; for it proves, I think, that the valley and foot-hill lands of California do not require for their profitable settlement either great estates or the help of great capitalists, as was formerly asserted, but that they can be most profitably and safely brought under culture by the co-operation of bodies of small landholders. It is the small farmers who make the state strong, wealthy, and prosperous; and one prosperous settlement like Riverside, or Anaheim, or Orange, or the Fresno Colony, or a dozen others, is worth a hundred great estates like those of Dr. Glenn, of Colusa, or of Miller & Lux in the San Joaquin Valley.

VIEW OF YOSEMITE FROM THE MARIPOSA TRAIL.

CHAPTER VII.

THE AGRICULTURAL LANDS AND PECULIARITIES OF CALIFORNIA.

THE singular variety of uses to which the soil of California lends itself for the farmer's benefit is even now but slowly being discovered. No year passes that some new culture is not introduced, or some old product produced on land before thought sterile or useless. The farmer here has had to invent many new methods, to adapt himself to the soil and climate, and it is no wonder that in the beginning an Eastern farmer thought this a sterile region, for it upsets all the Eastern ideas of farming.

In California the winter is the gala time of the year. The rains begin late in October. The grass is green and flourishing all winter; ploughing begins on the first of December; wheat, barley, oats, and other crops are sowed as soon as the land can be made fit; and sowing and planting are continued as late as February. Thus the husbandman has six or seven months to prepare his land for such a crop as wheat. Trees are also transplanted in this season. South of San Francisco, and in the San Joaquin Valley, frost is rarely known; roses bloom all the winter through; the flower-garden is constantly full of flowers; and south of the Tejon Pass many shade-trees, like the acacias, the pepper-tree, and the live-oaks, keep their foliage green the year round.

Corn is planted from March to May, and harvested as late as December. In the southern counties, and in the San Joaquin Valley especially, farmers take two crops from the same field—wheat or barley for the first, and corn for the second; and I have seen fields which yielded, in a good season, ninety bushels of corn for this second crop. Wheat and barley are commonly sown for hay, and in that case cut before the heads fill, in April or May. The harvest season for wheat, barley, and oats is in the latter part of May and in June.

After the middle of April the rains cease, and the whole harvest season is absolutely without rain. Thus the farmer is not hurried, and the grain harvest proceeds with none of that haste and anxiety about the weather which trouble the Eastern farmer. The small grains are usually gathered by a machine called a "header," which clips off only the heads of the grain stalk. Wheat, oats, and barley are threshed on the field, put into bags, and left, either on the field or along the railroad, for weeks often, in the open air, and until the crop is sold and shipped. The grain does not sweat, nor is it liable to injury from this exposure. Hay, too, is baled or stacked on the field, and left there until it is wanted. Potatoes are often left in the ground long after they are fit for digging. Thus it is evident the farmer has, in the long, dry California summer, an immense advantage over his Eastern competitor. He needs fewer hands, he is not hurried, and he requires no costly granaries or barns to shelter the products of his fields.

Nor does he need to put away much food for his cattle. A quarter of an acre of beets, replanted as they are used, will support two cows during the whole year. Work-horses receive barley and hay, but sheep are never fed; market cattle fatten in the pastures, and horses not at work get no food except what they pick up in the fields, in winter as well as summer. The alfalfa, or Chilian clover, which is now so largely sown, does well to feed to pigs, to cows, and even to plough-horses, and bears enormous crops. On low ground, or where it can be irrigated, as much as fifteen tons have been taken from an acre; it yields from six to nine cuttings in the year. Cattle and horses are more easily kept in condition in California than elsewhere in the United States, and the farmer needs no such substantial stables as in the Eastern States.

Fruit-trees bear much earlier than in the East. The peach bears a peck in the second year from planting the pit; the apple gives a crop at five years, and begins to bear at three; the curculio is unknown; and such perishable fruits as plums and cherries keep far longer than with us. I have eaten cherries and strawberries in Colorado which had been brought from Sacramento—a four days' journey—and they were in perfect order. The growth of fruit and other trees is extraordinary. The eucalyptus, a fine Australian evergreen shade-tree, has made twenty feet in a year, and I have seen one, eight years from a small cutting, which was seventy-five feet high and two feet in diameter at the base; the apricot becomes almost a forest-tree in size; and in the southern parts of the State it is the custom to make fences of sticks of willow, sycamore, or cotton-wood, cut to the length of eight feet, and stuck into the ground in December. These strike root at once, and grow so rapidly that in the second year the farmer cuts his fire-wood from these living fences.

Moreover, the variety of fruits cultivated in the farmer's orchard is much greater than with us. I have seen, commonly, in orchards, the apple, pear, peach, cherry, quince, prune, plum, nectarine, pomegranate—a most lovely tree or tall shrub when in bloom—the fig, which bears two crops a year; and in the southern part of the State the orange, lemon, lime, almond, olive, English walnut, and apricot; and you may eat strawberries, wherever care is bestowed upon them, in every month of the year. Fruit-trees are mostly free from disease, and the finest varieties of fruit known in the East grow freely here.

When you buy a farm in California you mostly buy open land. You have not to girdle trees, pull stumps, or toil among underbrush. Men do here more easily what they used to do in Illinois and Indiana—buy a farm, and with their first crop clear all their expenses and the price of the land. Where there are trees, except far up on the mountain-sides, they are usually the lovely oaks of this State, evergreen trees, which Nat-

AGRICULTURAL LANDS AND PECULIARITIES. 103

ure has planted so that the finest park-like effects are produced. I spent one 22d of February with a party of pleasant picnickers upon one of these oak-covered plains, green as our finest pastures are in June, with a lovely lake in the centre of a fair smooth field of about 1500 acres; with oaks scattered over the plain in irregular clumps and masses, and detached

VIEW NEAR THE STATE LINE, TRUCKEE RIVER.

trees, as beautifully as Olmsted or Vaux could place them; with finely rounded hills, green to their summits, surrounding us on every side; with skies so bright, and the air so mild and sweet, that a baby slept on the ground wrapped in shawls and rugs, and awoke rosy and crowing. It had rained hard overnight, but we sat on the greensward to eat our luncheon; and there were New Yorkers present rash and irreverent enough to declare that even the Central Park was never so lovely as this little piece of Nature's own landscape-gardening. The California live-oak is a low-branching, wide-spreading tree; it often attains the height of seventy feet, with a width—not circumference—of foliage of one hundred and twenty feet; and where it grows the plain is usually without underbrush—as clear and clean as a highly-cultivated park.

Where Nature has done and does so much man gains a quick reward for his efforts. Our costliest and rarest greenhouse flowers grow here out-of-doors all winter, almost without care. In the vineyards are planted by the acre the grapes which at home are found only in the hot-houses of the wealthy. The soil is so fertile, that it is a common saying in the great valleys that the ground is better after it has yielded two crops than at the first ploughing; and though, as a rule, the farmers in Southern California too often live in small and mean houses—the climate, which permits children to play out-of-doors without overcoats or shawls for at least 330 days in the year, and which makes the piazza or the neighboring shade-tree pleasanter than a room, in winter as well as summer—this is because one does not much need a house. The dwelling is a less important part of the farm than with us. The climate, even in the northern counties, does not oblige you to have a substantial or costly building; and while the farmer may and does work in the soil in every month in the year, and has thus an enormous advantage over his Eastern friend, on the other hand I do not exaggerate when I say that what a farmer in Iowa, Minnesota, or Kansas must pay out in two years for fuel to keep him and his family comfortable in winter, and for the shelter of his cattle from cold, would pay his way to California, and, if he chose well, almost buy him a farm.

To the settler from the far-off East it is an important advantage that California has, in a remarkable degree, a well-settled, orderly, and law-abiding population. Three races—the Indians, the old Spaniards, and we "Americans"—live there harmoniously together. No man need fear for his life or his property, even in the most thinly settled parts of the State.

Among the mountains of far-off San Bernardino County I found, ten years ago, a San Francisco lady established near a hot sulphur spring, and with but two children, the largest of them a boy of seventeen, building herself a house, employing carpenters and laborers, and "making" a place. She had found health and strength in this wilderness, and lived there without fear or danger.

For intelligent farmers—men who like to go a little out of the old ruts of farming—California seems to me the finest country conceivable.

I speak now especially of the great Sacramento and San Joaquin valleys, which contain the bulk of the richest farming land in the State. Such men may establish themselves by field crops; but they will find before them an almost illimitable field for experiment, with great rewards for perseverance and skill.

Near Marysville, a farmer, finding that his orchard of apples, pears, etc., did not pay as well as formerly, bethought him of the castor-bean. He planted several acres as an experimental crop, found that his soil was suitable for it, and I saw on his place one hundred acres in castor-oil. The plant, which is with us in the East a tender ornamental shrub, was planted and hoed or ploughed like corn, and, when ripe, a press in a shed at the edge of the field made the oil. In the East his adventure would have needed a solid brick building for his machinery, as well as costly drying and bleaching rooms. Here the oil was bleached under a rainless sky, and a shed which could not have cost fifty dollars sufficiently protected his engine and press.

In the Napa Valley a farmer thought hops would pay. He planted ten acres, and two crops gave him a handsome little fortune. Some years ago farmers within reach of the San Francisco market planted cherries; and I know a man whose cherry orchard, wherein Chinese pick the fruit at a trifling expense, has netted him for several years past thirty dollars a tree. Fine raisins are now made, and the manufacture of raisins has become within three or four years a highly profitable industry in Southern California.

Beet sugar has been successfully and profitably manufactured in several parts of the State, and the sugar-beet is found to yield a larger percentage of sugar in this climate than in France.

The silk culture has been successfully carried on in several parts of the State, and it would be more generally successful as an adjunct to other farming operations, where there are women and children to attend to this branch. Hops, of which I spoke above, obtain a higher price than those raised in the East, being stronger, and, owing to the dry summer, more sure to be gathered in good order. Flax and hemp are, on suitable soils, sure crops; and the culture of the ramie promises to be more profitable and successful in Southern California than elsewhere.

The vine, of course, grows well almost everywhere, and the best vineyardists are now planting German and French varieties, and trying to make light wines. But I believe in the San Joaquin and Tulare valleys the raisin grape will be found more profitable than even wine-making or brandy-distilling.

It is the great and uncommon variety of the agricultural products of California which surprises every one who examines the farming country. There is no region inhabited by English-speaking people, and having a well-settled government and a well-ordered society, in which this variety is anything like so great, or in which the arrangement of the seasons is so advantageous to the cultivator.

As I drove out from Los Angeles into the country on a January morning with a friend, we met a farmer coming into town with a market-wagon of produce.

It was a cloudless, warm, sunny day, and the plain where we met him was covered with sheep suckling their lambs, for in January it is already lambing time here. The farmer's little girl sat on the seat with him, a chubby, blue-eyed little tot, with her sun-bonnet half hiding her curls, and a shawl, which her careful mother had wrapped about her shoulders, carelessly flung aside. To me, fresh from the snowy Plains and Sierras, and with the chill breath of winter still on me, this was a pleasing and novel sight; but the contents of the man's wagon were still more startling to my Northern eyes. He was carrying to market oranges, pumpkins, a lamb, corn, green pease in the pod, lemons, and strawberries. What a mixture of Northern and Southern products! what an odd and wonderful January gathering in a farmer's wagon!

Around us the air was musical with the sweet sound of the baa-ing of young lambs. Surely there is no prettier or kindlier sight in the world than a great flock of peaceful, full-fed ewes, with their lambs, covering a plain of soft green as far as the eye can reach. All the fence corners, where there were fences, were crowded with the castor-oil plant, which is here a perennial, twenty feet high—a weed whose brilliant crimson seed-pods shine like jewels in the sunlight. Below us, as we looked from a hill-top, lay the suburbs of Los Angeles, green with the deep green of orange-groves, and golden to the nearer view with their abundant fruit. Twenty-one different kinds of flowers were blooming in the open air in a friend's garden in the town on that January day; among them the tuberose, the jasmine, and the fragrant stock or gillyflower, which has here a woody stalk, often four inches in diameter, and is, of course, a perennial. The heliotrope is trained over piazzas to the height of twenty feet; and though the apple and pear orchards, as well as those of the almond and English walnut, will continue bare for some time, and the vineyards, just getting pruned, look dreary, the vegetable gardens are green as with us in June, and men and boys are gathering the orange crop.

The finest varieties of grapes grow well in the northernmost counties of the State, and the prune, plum, and apricot are found to be nearly as profitable there as the orange, lemon, and olive farther south. The most successful wine makers in the State are now convinced that it is to the foot-hills of the Sacramento Valley, and in the northernmost counties of the State—regions where, as yet, but few vineyards have been planted —that they must look for the grapes which shall make the light and highest priced wines.

Fortunately for the State, it is now no longer doubted that small farms, ranging from as low as twenty to as high as eighty or one hundred

LAKE TAHOE.

and sixty acres, are the most profitable. There are still many great estates where wheat is grown by the cargo, or cattle range by the thousand; but it is a curious fact that the owners of many of these estates are constantly in debt. They are forced to rude and superficial culture; and while in what are good years they make a fortune, they contract expensive habits, and in bad years lose heavily. Meantime the increasing numbers of small farmers, in all parts of the State, are highly prosperous; many of them have in the last ten years acquired a handsome independence; and it is astonishing to see the improvements which have been made, in houses and grounds, in this period—the evidences, everywhere, of a sound and lasting prosperity among the farming community. One main reason for this is that on a small farm a great variety of crops can be made, by thorough culture, while the great estate owner runs his land to wheat alone, and, in fact, gambles, with the soil and the seasons as his counters.

What is the best and easiest way, you will perhaps ask, for an Eastern farmer to settle himself properly and safely in so far distant a State as California? The best and pleasantest way would be for four, six, or eight families to unite together, with the design to live on adjoining farms. Such a little association could send out one of their number as a pioneer to seek a suitable location. For four families a section of land would be sufficient. It would give each 160 acres of land. But if more is required, and if, for instance, it was desired to settle upon Government or railroad land in the Sacramento or San Joaquin Valley, it should be remembered that these are held in alternate sections (see diagram).

	Government Land. 640 Acres.	
Government Land. 640 Acres.	Railroad Land. 640 Acres.	Government Land. 640 Acres.
	Government Land. 640 Acres.	

Now so complete is the railroad land-office in San Francisco, that a stranger, coming to the State upon such an errand as I have supposed, would do best to go first to that office, look over its maps and descriptions of railroad "sections"—which can be purchased on five years' credit, with one-fifth paid down—and there, surveying the whole field at once, make up his mind what parts of it are best worth a more particular examination. A day or two in the railroad land-office would give him more information about the disposable land in California than a more tedious and costly search among the three or four Government land-offices located at different points, and each concerned with only a part of the State.

Having thus generally determined upon the part of the State which he thinks it best to examine, he will find it easy to make choice of some particular section or sections among those on his minutes.

In making his selection, he should bear in mind these things, among others:

1. California is subject to droughts. Experience shows, so far, that there are about seven good years out of ten; that is to say, in ten years

the farmer may, in almost any part of the State fit for general agriculture, expect to get seven good field crops without irrigation. This is the general testimony of careful and experienced farmers to whom I put the question. There are bottoms, as in the Pajaro Valley, and there are tracts of land in the northern part of the State and elsewhere, which are never affected by drought. But of the great bulk of the arable land in California what I have said above is true.

2. Moreover, the farmer in Southern California, who should plant the orange, lemon, almond, apricot, and other semi-tropical fruits, needs water to irrigate these.

3. Water is also needed, except in seasons when the rain-fall is above the average, to get two crops from the same land in a year. With water this is easy, and you may follow your crop of wheat or barley, sown in December and reaped in May, with a crop of corn planted in May or June, on the same land.

4. For all these reasons, it is a very great advantage to have a water supply on your place, or at least within reach. "Be more careful to buy water than land," said an experienced and successful California farmer to me—a man who, beginning with but a small capital fifteen years ago, has now an income of fifteen thousand dollars a year from his farm and orchards. Water is not scarce in California; and with it the farmer is independent of seasons, and has a control over his crops which is unknown elsewhere in the United States. The rainless summer and fall insures him fair weather for all his harvests—he needs no barn for hay or grain; none of the expensive "farm buildings" of an Eastern place; and by irrigation he kills the weeds, maintains his grasses, supports his crops, and it is very generally believed, even by scientific observers, increases the fertility of his land, because the water put on the surface dissolves the chemical constituents of the soil and prepares them for plant use.

5. There are now many new "Colony" settlements in the great valleys. The surprising success of the Anaheim, Riverside, and other colonies has given faith in these plans of settling the new lands. All these colonies began with an irrigation ditch; and where water is thus secured the price of land at once rises, often from two dollars and a half an acre to thirty or fifty dollars. There is still abundant room for colonies of Eastern or European farmers to secure cheap lands, and by a combined effort bring down water for their use. In such cases they easily assure their future. It is astonishing how small a stream answers every purpose; and to an Eastern man few things are more surprising than the ease, skill, and cheapness with which a small stream is tapped by half a

hundred California farmers, according to a plan matured at a "ditch-meeting," and made available for irrigation. Concerning methods and cost of irrigation I shall give some details in a subsequent chapter, as well as concerning the colony method of settlement, which has achieved such surprising successes in this State.

"PROSPECTING."

6. The level or plain land is probably the richest; it is certainly the most easily cultivated, and it comes first into use. But the foot-hills have a peculiar value of their own, which has been overlooked by the eager California farmers. The vine and the semi-tropical fruits grow best in or near the foot-hills. The soil will probably not bear such heavy crops of grain; but a homestead on the hills has a fine lookout; water is more easily obtainable; the air is fresher than on the plains; and, for my own part, I have seen, in the more settled parts of the State, that the cheapest lands—namely, the foot-hill lands—were, on many accounts, preferable. Vine-growers perceive that the best wine comes from these higher lands; and fifteen years hence it is believed that the principal and most profitable vineyards in the State will be in the foot-hills.

7. California is a breezy State; the winds from the sea draw with considerable force through the cañons or gorges in the mountains and sweep over the plains. This is, no doubt, one of the chief causes of its remarkable healthfulness; and it gives to the workman, in the summer, the great boon of cool nights. No matter how warm the day has been in any part of the State, the night is always cool, and a heavy blanket is needed for comfort. Now, there are places where the wind is too severe, where a constant gale sweeps through some cañon, and is an injury to the farmer. Such places should be avoided, and are easily avoidable. In many parts of the State farms are now systematically surrounded by plantations of trees, planted as wind-breaks; and, fortunately, the willow or sycamore forms, in two years, in this climate, a sufficient shelter, besides furnishing fire-wood to the farmer.

"PANNING OUT."

8. Where one man has selected land for himself and several friends, he can easily and quickly prepare the way for them. Fences and houses can be built by contract in every part of the State. Men make it their business to do this; and at the nearest town the intending settler can always have all his necessary "improvements" done by contract, even to

ploughing his land and putting in his first crop. In this respect labor is admirably organized in California. You will see, then, that your pioneer may make ready for those who are to come after, so as to save them much delay and inconvenience.

9. As the winter in the Northern States is said to be the best time to see the country if you mean to buy, so the summer and fall are the best seasons for a farmer to visit California, if he thinks of settling there. After May there is no rain until November. This makes a long, dry season, in which many of the smaller streams dry up, the pastures become brown and look bare, the roads are dusty, and whatever is disagreeable in climate or country comes out to the surface. Fortunately, during this period also the harvest takes place and the fruits are ripening, so that not only the dust and dryness, but the fruitfulness and wealth of the land, are seen. Moreover, if you select your land in summer or fall, you are just in time to have your crop put in when the rains begin.

10. Thus it is possible and easy for one person coming out during the summer or fall not only to select lands for a party of friends or neighbors, but to have their houses built, their fences — if they need any — made, and their first crops put in, by contract; so that when the families come out in November or December all would be prepared for them, and they would have only to move in, and during the first winter to make vegetable gardens, put in alfalfa, beets, and corn fodder for their cattle, and set out their orchards. The roads are generally good all winter; the rains do not last long, and the bright sun quickly dries up the mud; and there is no "freeze and thaw" to break up the roads, as in our Northern States.

A CALIFORNIA VINEYARD.

CHAPTER VIII.

GRAPES AND WINE.

WHO drinks California wine? Evidently somebody drinks it, for there is an immense quantity of it made. In 1880 the wine-crop amounted to over ten million gallons; and in the same year, so profitable are vineyards, ten thousand new acres were planted to vines. The product of California's vineyards, in wine, brandy, market grapes, and raisins, was valued that year at over three millions of dollars. The export of wine from the State was about two and a half million gallons, with 189,000 gallons of brandy.

It is, in fact, a great industry; and it has, happily, been systematized in the past ten years in such way that the vineyardist is no longer compelled to make his own wine, but may now almost everywhere sell his grapes to a wine-maker. The wine grapes are sold to the manufacturer by the ton; and the presses, cellars, casks, and other costly apparatus needed to turn the grapes into wine fit for the market are, as they ought to be, the property of capitalists, firms who have the means, which farmers have not, to enable them to manufacture and to mature and market their product to advantage. In the early days, and, indeed, until quite recently, the owner of a vineyard was obliged to have also a cellar, casks, presses, and needed, therefore, a considerable capital—more than a farmer usually has; and there is no doubt that, while this worked badly and oppressively on the vine-raisers, it also made vine-culture a business by which many a poor farmer and his boys became sots. It is not good for everybody to spend much time in a wine-cellar; and in the first edition of this book I advised new settlers not to plant vineyards, for this reason, that having to make wine would expose many of them to contracting habits of intemperance and tippling. The great change which has come about in the management of the business avoids this danger. The farmer who sells his grapes to a wine-maker has no more temptation to wine-bibbing than if he sold grain to the mill.

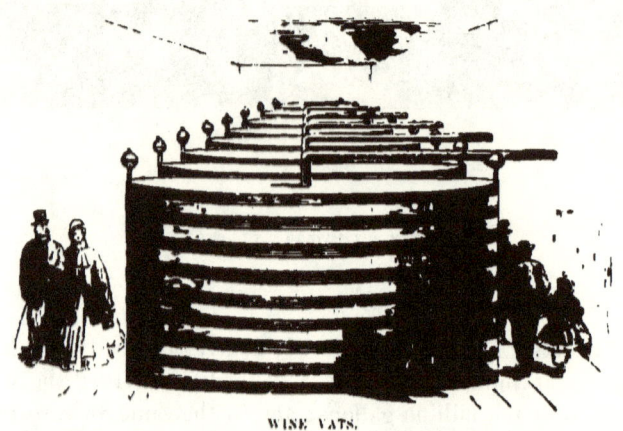

WINE VATS.

How largely capital has gone into the business of making wine may be judged from the fact that there are now numerous wine-presses in the State, at which from eight to ten tons of grapes are stemmed and crushed in an hour; and there are cellars attached to these presses which hold casks of a capacity of three thousand gallons each, while there are casks in such cellars which hold from ten thousand to fourteen thousand gallons each.

The price of grapes varies from year to year, as with other crops. In 1879 they brought, at the wine centres, mission grapes from $14 to $16 per ton; and for the finer varieties from $18 to $26 per ton. It is reckoned that a vineyard should bear four tons to the acre—some bear more than this, especially in the southern part of the State, and where the vine is irrigated. I should think three and a half tons to the acre a fair crop, although I have seen a vineyard bear ten tons per acre. The wine-makers complain that the prices of 1879 were too high, and I have no doubt that they were; and that prices will, as a rule, be considerably lower than these. Nevertheless, prices are well maintained this year; for those agreed on and publicly announced in the several viticultural districts into which the State has been divided are even higher than two years ago. In Sonoma, Napa, and Stockton, mission grapes—the common grape of the country—now chiefly used for brandy and heavy wines, brought

TRAINING THE VINE.

$25 per ton in the fall of 1881; foreign varieties, $30; Zinfandel, from which claret is made, $30 to $32; and Riesling, the grape for white wines and champagnes, $30 to $35 at the wineries. In the Los Angeles country $20 per ton was paid for mission, and $25 per ton for foreign grapes, and similar prices in other parts of the State.

The establishment of wineries has placed the vineyard interest of the State on permanent and safe ground. Capital finds good returns in this business, for the market for California wines increases constantly and rapidly; and the best wine-makers in the State already see that it will pay them to keep large stocks of their best product on hand to mature, and thus largely increase its value. Ten years ago there was no California claret worthy of the name of wine; now New Orleans consumes annually many thousand casks of California claret, and it finds a market also in the Eastern cities. It begins to be understood that the wines of California do improve with age, and with the increasing skill of the wine-makers, while it is undeniable that they are pure juice of the grape, prepared by far cleaner and more perfect methods than are used anywhere in Europe. The grapes here are unsoiled by the human touch after they are picked, as they are stemmed and crushed by machinery, and in most of the wineries—so abundant is the juice—the wine is made only of that juice which drains of itself from the crusher. That the wine so made is rapidly opening a wider market for itself is evident from the statistics of the trade. In 1875 California exported out of the State a little over a million gallons of wine; four years later the export had reached 2,155,944 gallons—that is to say, it had more than doubled. In 1880 the export was 2,487,353 gallons of wine, besides 189,000 gallons of brandy. That the wines of California are taking the place of European wines in America is equally clear from statistics. The import into the United States of French wines, in 1874, was over five and a quarter million gallons; in 1878 it had fallen to less than half this amount. Meantime, the failure of French vineyards continues and increases, as is shown by the heavy increase in the importation of foreign wines into France. France imports wine in large quantities from various countries—chiefly Spain, Portugal, Austria, Italy, and Turkey; and from these five countries she took, in 1879, 7,287,376 American gallons, and in nine months of 1880, 14,652,000 American gallons. Mr. Haraszthy, of San Francisco, the chief California authority on wine culture, says that if California should plant vineyards at the rate of ten thousand acres per annum, it would require a century for the State to possess as many acres of vines as have been destroyed by phylloxera in France in the last eight years. France has lost over a million acres of grapes by vine disease; California has but 85,000 acres planted in vines, of which 20,000 acres are new vines, and have not yet borne. It is clear that this industry is still but in its infancy in the State, and that it has a very wide and lasting future.

This is seen by the capitalists of the State; and one hears on all hands, and in a dozen counties, of men of wealth planting out from 100 to 1000 acres in vines as a profitable and permanent investment. For my part, I do not believe these great vineyards will, in the long-run, be pecuniarily successful. The vine needs more care than will be given to it in these large vineyards, where the owner's eye is absent, and must be replaced by careless foremen and uninterested laborers. The small vineyards will be the profitable ones; and the possessor of forty or even twenty acres will secure a handsome profit, and keep his vines strong and healthful, while the vines on the great estates will slowly perish, and never bear satisfactorily. It is the small vineyards in the foot-hills of the Sacramento Valley which will some day bear off the great prizes in wine culture, and become permanently profitable properties. Fortunately for the men of small means coming into the State, these lands are still the cheapest in the State. The foot-hill country of the southern counties, on the other hand, will be, I believe, the great raisin-producing region of the world, for the dryer climate and the hotter sun of this great district has been within two or three years discovered to be peculiarly favorable to the highest development and cheapest preparation of the raisin-grape. But of this I reserve details for a special chapter.

The best vine land in the State is not yet planted to vines. It is in the foot-hills of the northern counties, whose climate approaches more nearly that of the great wine region of Germany and France, that the finest wines of the State will some day be grown. Irrigation is not necessary in these northern counties, and it is now generally acknowledged that irrigation, while it increases the crop, somewhat deteriorates the quality of the grape. The foot-hills of the Sierra, north of Marysville, and as far north as the State line, will before very long be the great wine country of California, and land in those parts is still abundant and cheap. It is to the northern half of the Sacramento Valley that I should recommend new settlers to turn their attention who mean to grow the vine. Southward, in the San Joaquin Valley, the raisin-grape will, as I have said, prove equally profitable, and more certain of good results.

Land of approved quality for vineyards can be bought at various prices, from five to one hundred dollars per acre. In those counties where the culture has been long established the prices are the highest, but there is much land, capable of producing the very best quality of wine, which can still be obtained for from five to ten dollars per acre, and in small or great quantities; and this quality of land is, in the opinion of the most competent judges in the State, by far the best for the finest varieties of grapes, making the best and most costly wines.

A BOTTLING-CELLAR.

The vine grows so healthily in most parts of California that it suffers very little from disease and animal pests. Phylloxera is found in the old vine districts, but it does not seem to spread. It is believed that irrigation serves as a check upon it; but the careful investigations of the Viticultural Society, while they make this probable, do not appear to show so serious and heroic a remedy necessary. I do not doubt that in the great vineyards planted and badly managed by capitalists disease will make dangerous headway, but the small holders do not, it would seem, need to fear disastrous or even troublesome results.

When I say that the average product of vineyards in the State is about three and a half tons of grapes to the acre. I must add that in many considerable districts this average is largely exceeded; and from eight to ten tons per acre is not an uncommon crop, where irrigation is practised. I believe the product is greatest in the southern counties; but also, for the finer and lighter wines, it is least valuable there. For brandy, however, the southern grapes are very useful.

"CRADLE-ROCKING."

CHAPTER IX.

RAISIN-MAKING.

TEN years ago Californians produced in limited quantities an article called "dried grapes," which was sold in the mining camps and among the poor as a cheap substitute for raisins. "Dried grapes" were usually dried mission grapes; they would not keep, would not bear transportation to long distances, were not soundly cured, and, in short, were not raisins. The product was of no commercial importance. Two years ago the California raisin product amounted to perhaps 200,000 dollars. Next year it will be worth half a million; and unless, for some reason not now apparent, it receives a check, California will in ten years supply a large part of the raisins of commerce. It is one of the most promising and important of the recently introduced industries in this State.

Mr. R. B. Blowers, of Woodland, in Yolo County, deserves most of the credit of introducing and perfecting the raisin culture in California; he is now, in 1882, the largest single producer in the State; and many of those farmers who have begun successfully to make raisins acknowledge that they have copied the methods which his careful experiments have shown the best, and which, to his credit, he has most liberally imparted to them.

The muscatel Gordo Blanco is the raisin-grape of California, as it is of Spain. It is the most delicious table-grape grown in California; it has been used as a wine grape, and is still used in the production of brandy. But it will now, and for years to come, be cultivated chiefly for raisins. It is as easily grown, and as hardy, as any of the other varieties, and so far, I think, even freer from disease; the thrips being, as far as I have heard, its chief enemy. It bears irrigation remarkably well, and irrigation kills its enemies. Mr. Blowers uses water very freely in his raisin vineyard, and told me that last winter he kept his vines during nearly four weeks covered two feet deep with water. His belief is that this, which looks like heroic treatment, kills all insect plagues, as well as anything of the phylloxera kind; that the irrigation stream leaves a deposit in the vineyard which serves as the most valuable manure, and that it increases the yield and does not injure the flavor of the grape. Certainly the results I saw in the present year confirmed this theory. But, although the soil of his vineyard is naturally rich, he does not depend entirely on that and the sedimentary deposit from irrigation, but applies other manures, especially bone-dust and ashes. Stable manure he and others have found to be too coarse for the vine.

The chief feature, however, of his method, is the most thorough culture with plough, harrow, cultivator, and other tools, to keep the surface soil absolutely clear of weeds, and in a loose and mellow condition; and as this chapter may interest farmers, I will add that I am satisfied that for the climate and soils of California this clean and thorough culture is more important than anything else, and I almost venture to say than all else, the farmer can do to secure a large crop of any product. Water is valuable, and in many parts indispensable; just now one may see thousands of acres blossoming and fruitful, on which water has been led, and which, before that, were denounced as unmitigated and irreclaimable desert. But there are only too many spots where one sees that water is misused by an idle or careless farmer who neglects the plough and cultivator; and here he gets only a rank growth of weeds, and a stunted and diseased growth of his crops and trees. The best and most successful farmers in the driest parts of California have assured me, without exception, that after the first soaking of the virgin soil—which requires, of course, a large quantity of water—surprisingly little is needed for annual irrigation, if only the ground is thoroughly prepared, and constantly kept loose and clean.

RAISIN-MAKING.   121

Thus, Mr. Blowers told me that he goes through his vineyard with various tools used for cleaning and loosening the soil as many as sixteen times in the year. But, also, he assured me that the average product of his vineyard, for the last six years, was six tons of grapes to the acre, which is, he says, the equivalent of two tons of marketable raisins; and

INDIAN RANCHERIA.

he has got as high as two and a half tons of raisins to the acre. The most perfect culture also secures the largest grapes and most perfect bunches; and he added, as the result of his experience, that the poorer qualities sell at so much lower prices as make the best and, of course, most costly culture the most profitable by far.

All vines bear quickly in the favorable climate of this State, granted proper care. In Fresno County, on irrigated land, I have seen many vines which bore several large bunches of grapes the same year in which they were planted as "rooted cuttings." Mr. Blowers gave me as his experience and that of others, that a vineyard of the raisin-grape, carefully cultivated, and with irrigation, should yield enough in the third year to pay for all the labor put upon it in that year, including the picking; and that in the fourth year it should repay, and in many cases within his knowledge has repaid, the entire cost of land, planting, and culture up to that time; even where the land has cost originally as much as a hundred dollars per acre. But it is well known that a vine is not in full bearing until the seventh, or even the tenth year after planting. To plant and cultivate a raisin vineyard should cost, to the time of bearing, not less than forty dollars per acre, probably more—this exclusive of picking and curing the grapes, of course. On the other hand, he told me he had made raisins where they yielded a dollar for every vine to the acre—five hundred and fifty being the number usually planted per acre. He thought good raisin land, with water secured, would be reasonable in price at from \$80 to \$125 per acre; but this, I judge, would include such nearness to market as his own neighborhood. Certainly, there is a vast quantity of good land in the southern part of the State, in the San Joaquin Valley, Los Angeles and San Bernardino counties, obtainable and suitable for this crop, at from twenty to forty dollars per acre, with water secured; and without water ditches, but lying in large tracts, where a body of settlers could bring water by a united effort, such land can still be got, at from five to ten dollars per acre, in parts where both climate and soil are the most favorable for the raisin-grape.

In several vineyards I have seen the seedless or sultana grape growing to perfection, and raisins are successfully made of it, though as yet in small quantities. It is an enormous bearer when properly trimmed; but was thought at first to be a failure, because the true method of treating it was not known. The Zante currant also grows well, but its culture has not yet been successful.

Until the past fall (1881) the comparatively few farmers who cultivated the raisin-grape have made their own raisins. The process is not difficult; nor does it require, south of Stockton, any complicated or costly machinery. The sun, by universal consent, is the best dryer; and artificial drying, where it is resorted to, is found to make a poorer quality of raisins. The grape-bunches are carefully cut from the vine, defective grapes removed, and the bunches then laid either upon the ground—which I found the general practice in Los Angeles County—or upon trays of board, about three feet square, which should be tilted up slightly toward the sun by placing a clod of earth under one end. Here the grapes lie until the upper or exposed surface is tolerably dry. They must then be turned, and this must be done with as little handling or disturbing of the grapes as possible. They need to be turned but once; but in localities liable to sea-fogs or rain they should be covered at night.

When sufficiently cured they are still unequally dried, some grapes in a bunch being very dry, others less so. At the proper stage they are brought into a house, and laid in "sweat-boxes," which are open boxes four feet square and two and a half or three feet deep; and these being piled on top of each other, the grapes, now already raisins, are left there for a sufficient time, from a day to four or five days, to allow the moisture remaining unequally distributed to permeate the whole mass of raisins; those which were over-dry drawing from those which had an excess of moisture left. This is the final process before packing; and the whole is, you will observe, sufficiently simple, and indeed primitive, requiring only a little judgment, experience, and care. A lady who farms quite successfully in Fresno County (Miss Austin, of the Central Colony), showed me excellent raisins of her own curing, and told me that she had but little experience, but had used proper care and judgment, and found herself satisfactorily successful.

Farmers in Los Angeles County believed that the better way was to dry the raisin on the ground, and not on the board trays used elsewhere. The heat retained by the soil was a help during the cool nights which here obtain, they thought. They certainly had fair-looking raisins; but to me the exposure on clean boards seemed nicer and safer.

The wine culture lagged until large wineries were established, at which grapes are bought from the farmers at a fixed rate per ton. That feature is at the base of the recent great success of wine-making and vine culture in this State. It is probable that, as the planting of the raisin-grape becomes more general in the southern half of the State, where climate and soil especially favor it, the farmers will in like manner be able to sell their raisin-grapes, either in the field or dried, to men who will make a business of drying and packing them. In a part of Los Angeles County I found this useful and convenient subdivision of labor already going on, though not yet in a systematic or settled way. Some farmers had sold their grapes on the vine to men who undertook the picking, drying, and packing; others had dried their grapes, and then sold them by the ton to professional packers, which was an undoubted convenience. But this subdivision of labor is still in its infancy, and needs to be systematized.

It is at the Colony of Riverside, near San Bernardino, that the raisin culture has been prosecuted most extensively and successfully, and there the returns, for such general culture as is given by the average farmer, were shown to me to be from one hundred to two hundred dollars per acre, net profit; those who packed their own raisins and gave special care and skill to the drying and packing making as much as $250 clear per acre. The difference between one hundred and two hundred dollars per acre depended on the age of the raisin vineyards; and none in Riverside, or, indeed, elsewhere in the State, are as yet old enough to be in full bearing.

THE MEXICAN ARASTRA.

CHAPTER X.

SEMI-TROPICAL FRUITS.

ONE of the most important crops of the southern half of California promises to be the crop of what are called citrus fruits — the orange, lemon, and lime. In the localities where these do well, but also over a much greater part of the State, several others, the almond, English walnut, and olive, are also very profitable.

Since the first edition of this book was issued, in 1872, the culture of these fruits has become general, and a large mass of experience has been gained by farmers and orchardists, very valuable and important to persons now proposing to plant. Ten years ago it was not believed that grafting or budding would improve the orange, and there was, in fact, but one variety of either this fruit or the lemon in the State. Now a dozen varieties of each are known, and the orchardist shows you the peculiarities of each, and its merits for eating or for market; while it has become an object to discover the most favorable localities for planting, where the fruit will ripen earliest, and where the tree is least subject to disease.

Formerly it was thought necessary to irrigate the orange and lemon trees as often as once in six weeks. Now the best opinion is that four or five applications of water in the year are sufficient, and maintain the tree in a healthier condition. Formerly it was thought that an orange orchard could not be made to yield a profit under ten years; now, by the method of budding, dwarf trees are produced which begin to bear in five years from the bud, and yield paying crops in six years. Farther experience is required to establish whether these budded trees will be as long lived or as full bearing as seedlings and standards; but they seem, at any rate, to shorten the period of waiting for a profitable orchard.

In short, a large mass of experience in the culture of all the fruits I have spoken of above has been gained in the last ten years, and of what I wrote in the earlier editions concerning the culture of semi-tropical fruits little remains true or correct, excepting only the statements I there made concerning the remarkable profitableness of this culture. These statements the experience of the last ten years has entirely confirmed, as I will show farther on in this chapter. Before passing to the class called "citrus fruits" I will speak of the almond, English walnut, and olive.

The almond has, so far, made but a moderate success in California. There are now almond orchards in several parts of the State ten or twelve years old — old enough to yield full crops. The general testimony of almond growers is that the tree is an abundant bearer when it bears at all, but that its habit seems to be shy and uncertain. Why it should be so no one I saw could tell me. A successful grower in Yolo County, whose almond orchard of nine thousand trees bore well this past fall, told me that he had had but a meagre crop for the three previous years, why he could not tell, for he had given the trees excellent care. He remarked that last spring he had noticed great numbers of bees about the trees — and thought it possible that these were needed to fertilize the fruit blossoms. Another almond grower in the southern part of the State thought the tree needed longer time to come into full bearing than had been allowed it in the general opinion. But he had rooted out most of his almonds, and planted oranges and lemons in their places, as more certain and much more profitable.

Mr. Saul, the experienced manager of a large orchard near Davisville, in Yolo County, told me that the almonds, in his care, began to bear the fourth year, and should bear good crops after the sixth year — say from ten to twenty pounds per tree. He had this year what he thought a good crop, several thousand trees yielding an average of fifteen pounds of marketable fruit per tree. He had harvested his crop, and was hulling and bleaching them, and the price at that time was fourteen cents per pound. The cost of picking, hulling, bleaching, and sacking he reckoned at three and a half cents per pound; and I suppose ten cents a pound would be the net profit, which would give $1 50 per tree, or, at 150 trees to the acre, $225 clear profit per acre.

The machinery needed for hulling is very simple, an inexpensive huller having been invented, which is moved by horse-power. The bleaching is done with the fumes of sulphur, in an air-tight storehouse, so arranged that the sulphur vapor can reach the almonds, which are laid on lattice-work shelves. The favorite variety has a moderately hard shell; this is thought to be the most profitable for marketing. The paper-shell they say breaks up too easily in handling, and thus entails losses, or else necessitates more careful and expensive handling.

In some parts of the State it has been found that the hull sticks to a part of the almonds in such way that the huller does not take it off. Where this happens it is the custom to crack the nut and market only the kernel; and for this a lower price is received.

I judge from all I heard that the almond has not become a favorite tree in the southern part of the State; but that its main success will be in sheltered localities north of Sacramento, and more, probably, in the foot-hills than on the plains. I should say, also, that it is more likely to succeed away from the ocean, than where the tree is exposed to even a little sea-fog. Its safe northern limit has not yet been found. It will grow and do well as far as Chico, in the Sacramento Valley, and probably all over Northern California in well-selected spots. I suspect that the summer heat of the southern counties may be unfavorable to its regular bearing.

The olive has proved a success in only a few hands. It is a slow bearer, and it has been attacked by several enemies wherever it has been planted in Southern California. Mr. Elwood Cooper, near Santa Barbara, has the largest and most successful bearing orchard in the State; and he has found it very profitable. He began to make olive oil in 1880, and found an urgent demand for all his crop, at prices which realized, he told me, all his expectations of the great value of these trees. Mr. Cooper is the chief authority in the State on the olive culture, and he asserts that the tree will succeed safely, if only it has sufficient care. His own extensive orchards certainly look well. The trees are clean and healthy, and those in bearing were full of olives. Colonel Hollister, near Santa Barbara, has also large and flourishing olive orchards; and near San

Diego there are several others. Elsewhere I found the olive planted only in small numbers; though near Los Angeles there are several old and successful orchards. I have no doubt the earlier maturity and greater profitableness of the citrus fruits, and of the apricot, prune, and peach, have made men shy of planting olive orchards.

That the tree does well, with proper care, there is no doubt, and the quality of the fruit is excellent. Mr. Cooper's olive oil has already a fame of its own in the Eastern States; and he and others who now make oil could sell much more than they produce. The pickled olives of California are the most delicious I have eaten. They are not found, so far as I know, out of the State, but are favorites in the best private houses and restaurants in San Francisco, and will be preferred to French or Spanish olives by all who have a real taste for this delicacy. The art of pickling them begins to be very well understood in several places, especially about Los Angeles.

It is not easy to state, with certainty, the profits of an olive orchard. The general opinion is that olives will prove as profitable as oranges, and that a bearing orchard will yield from five to seven hundred dollars per acre net profit; the cost of care, picking, and oil-making being somewhat more than that of marketing oranges or lemons.

The English walnut is also one of the profitable crops of California. It will do well in almost all parts of the State; and is one of the trees which should be planted by most farmers in their borders or in pastures, for when it matures it is like a forest-tree, hardy and requiring little care. It matures very slowly, like most of the nut-trees; begins to bear at about eight years, and does not give a full crop until fifteen years old. Some orchards twelve and thirteen years old bear now, about Los Angeles and Santa Barbara, at the rate of $200 to $350 per acre net profit, and this with very little care, as the tree is not subject to the attacks of insects or disease. The gopher and ground squirrel are its chief enemies; they attack the roots of the young trees. My belief is that this tree will make the most rapid growth in rather moist soil, and that where alfalfa is grown, which has to be frequently irrigated, the English walnut would succeed, if planted in the borders or along the water ditches. The quality of the California nut is very good.

I come finally to the citrus fruits — the orange, lemon, and lime. These are now planted on a large scale in several parts of the State, and especially in Los Angeles and San Bernardino counties, where they will before long form one of the chief crops. Their culture has been prosecuted with much intelligence, with the result that the area of suitable soil has been widened, and new and earlier-bearing varieties have been introduced or created. The region suitable to the profitable culture of the citrus fruits has by no means been fully explored. They do not at present succeed on the San Joaquin and Sacramento plains, and may never be a profitable crop there; though with shelter and care, with wind-breaks to protect the garden, and skilful treatment, I believe the farmers on those plains will be able to easily raise oranges enough for their own consumption. The frosts, which now seem to them to put the orange out of the range of their climate and locality, are no more dangerous to this tree than the frosts of a large part of our Middle States are to the peach.

But in the foot-hills, both in the San Joaquin and the Sacramento valleys, the orange and lemon already do well, and can safely be planted. As this great foot-hill region, now containing the cheapest and best lands in the State, and the loveliest situations, becomes settled by small farmers, it will be discovered that here is the real and best fruit country of California. I do not mean to be understood as saying that the northern limit of the citrus fruits in the foot-hills will reach very far north of Sacramento; but there is a great extent of country whose capabilities are as yet almost untried and unknown, in which the orange will bear, at least for home consumption, and where the prune, the apricot, the peach, plum, and cherry will be the great market crops; some of them almost as profitable as the orange; and all bearing very much earlier.

Oranges sell in the California market nowadays for from ten to sixty dollars per thousand, the very great difference being caused by earliness in the market, and by difference in quality.

The seedling orange-tree bears, at twelve years from the planting, an average of 1000 marketable oranges, and I know of a tree at Riverside which bore at thirteen years 2250 oranges, which brought the owner seventy-four dollars. The following year—namely, in 1880—it bore 2050. The orange is prone to overbear, and this tree had evidently done too much, for in 1881 it had less than half this number of oranges on it.

They plant from eighty to one hundred trees per acre; and it is easy to see that the profits of a bearing orchard, even at the lowest prices, are very great. Eighty trees, bearing 1000 oranges each, sold at ten dollars per thousand, would yield a gross return of $800. Now, one man can cultivate, irrigate, prune, and care for twenty acres of any of the citrus fruits, and the picking and boxing cost no more than about $1.50 per thousand. But at fifteen years old seedling-trees bear 2000 oranges each, and the average price of a crop is now, and will for many years remain, over twenty dollars per thousand. The trees are long-lived, where they have good care, and in proper localities are not subject to serious diseases. But they require thorough and constant culture; and the man who lets weeds dispute the ground with his trees, or who allows the soil to bake about the roots, will soon find his orchard diseased.

Lemons, where the best varieties are cultivated, are as surely and largely profitable as oranges. The lime is also a very profitable fruit. Lemon-trees need, I am told, to be planted in sheltered localities to do well.

The practice of budding oranges and lemons has in a measure revolutionized this culture, because budded roots bear much earlier, yielding a moderately profitable crop at five years; and the best and highest priced varieties are grown on budded stocks. And on such an assured basis is this culture now, that in localities where the orange and lemon are known to do well, as at Orange and San Gabriel in Los Angeles County, and at Riverside in San Bernardino County, orange land is now readily sold at two hundred dollars and over per acre—with water, of course—and is not thought dear at that price. Before its use was established, the same land, subdivided for colony settlements, and with water brought to it, was thought high-priced at thirty-five dollars per acre.

Is not the market likely to be overstocked? I do not believe it. Its area is constantly widening. I saw Riverside grapes going to Kansas; pears from the country about Sacramento are shipped to Chicago by many car-loads; and the orange and lemon will bear much farther transportation than either grapes or pears.

When I first wrote on this subject, in 1871, the question of the permanent and very great profitableness of the citrus fruits in California was still open; but it is now settled. One of the shrewdest orchardists at Riverside said to me, "At half a cent apiece the orange crop would still remain the most profitable a man could grow;" and he was right. Half a cent each would be five dollars per thousand; which for mature trees would still give a gross return of ten dollars to the tree, or from $800 to $1000 per acre, according to the number of trees planted per acre in different localities.

Such returns seem incredible, even to one on the ground; and I needed, to enable me to realize the practical results, some such statement as was made to me by one of the most careful and intelligent orange cultivators I met—the owner of twenty acres in a choice location. "Last year my trees paid the whole of my family expenses for the year; that was my first crop. This year I shall make over five thousand dollars clear; after next year I am planning to take my family for six months to Europe, and I expect thereafter to have four or five months for travel every year, with sufficient means from my twenty acres to go where my wife and children may wish to go."

For the result thus described he had labored, with no severe toil, for nine years, in a delightful climate; and I could not but compare his fortunes with those of a professional man or merchant—not to speak of an Eastern farmer—toiling severely for an equal number of years, with small hope of any such results.

COAST VIEW, MENDOCINO COUNTY.

CHAPTER XI.

CANNING AND DRYING FRUITS.

ONE of the new industries developed in California, to the great profit of its small farmers and orchardists, is the canning and drying of fruits.

The apricot, prune, plum, cherry, and pear are the fruits which have obtained, when preserved or dried, the widest and most profitable markets. All these trees do well, are hardy, thrifty, and bear abundantly in almost all parts of the State; and the market for them, wherever what are called "canning factories" are established, is such that a profit of from $100 to $200 per acre for a bearing orchard can be counted on by the farmer.

I was surprised to find that some of the fruit canneries prepare their goods entirely for European markets. One manager told me that he had shipped the whole product of the season—largely canned apricots and muscat grapes—to London, where he had orders for all he could produce. Another had found his market in Germany, and shipped direct there, without the intervention of a middle-man. The demand for these "canned" fruits is rapidly increasing, and California has almost a monopoly of the market for many varieties, especially for the apricot.

The climate of California appears to be especially suited to this tree. It begins to bear the third year after planting out from nursery rows; it is, so far, free from disease, bears abundantly, and grows to so great a size, that I have seen single specimens which had the appearance of half-grown forest-trees. It has but recently come into general cultivation, and I do not doubt will continue, for a long time to come, one of the most profitable of the orchard trees of California. It does well in all the valleys, as well as in the foot-hills. Its congener, the nectarine, has more lately come into orchard use, and less is known about it.

Next to the apricot, I think the prune is the most promising of the deciduous fruit-trees. It has been introduced but a few years, but promises well wherever it has been tried. The plum also bears well; and dried plums, as well as dried pears, bring such a price in the market as to make these crops very profitable.

It must be understood that they dry these fruits only where they are too far from market to tempt shipment as fresh fruit. About Sacramento and Stockton there are numerous orchards and vineyards where grapes, and pears, plums, and other fruits, are grown for shipment to the East, fresh; and this is one of the most profitable farming operations in the State. The orchardist or vineyardist does not himself ship the fruit; two or three Chicago firms have undertaken this business, and this simplifies the farmer's work greatly, as well as saves him the outlay of a large working capital. At one orchard, not far from Sacramento, I saw hundreds of bushels of pears gathered under a large shed. They had been sold in bulk for three cents per pound to a Chicago firm, who themselves undertook the whole charge and cost of packing them for market. Thus the orchardist had no labor except to pick the fruit and deposit it under the shed, except that he had also engaged to haul the boxes to the railroad station near by. As the orchard was large there was a quantity of windfalls, and these were getting pared and cut up by machinery, were then dried in the sun, and found a market as "dried pears," being in ready demand at good prices. The same manner of marketing is pursued with plums; and the cherry is one of the most profitable orchard crops in California, because, unlike our Eastern cherry, it bears transportation and will keep in good condition for several days. I have eaten California cherries in Denver at least five or six days from the tree, and in good condition.

The business of canning and drying fruits is still in its infancy in California. It is destined to a great development; and the preserved fruits of this State, which have already made their way to European markets, will in a few years be in demand over a considerable part of the world. The canneries give employment to a large number of women and children, and the business, as I have seen it carried on in different parts of the State, is well systematized and intelligently conducted, with the help of labor-saving machinery. The "canneries" are well aired, the fruit is carefully selected, and an admirable cleanliness and order prevail in them. Only the best materials are used—the fruit is so abundant and cheap, that there is no temptation to use stale or poor qualities; and the canneries are always placed in the midst of an orchard region, so that the fruit is not injured by long transportation. I did not wonder, when I saw the care taken with the fruit, that the product has rapidly grown into favor in Europe as well as at home.

WOOD-CHOPPER AT WORK.

CHAPTER XII.

ALFALFA.

ALFALFA is lucern, under another—a Chilian or Spanish—name. Its introduction into California dates not more than fifteen years back, and will some day be accounted as one of the important steps in making agriculture a legitimate industry in the State, instead of a vulgar and hazardous speculation.

The introduction of new grasses into a country is one of the most valuable aids its agriculture can receive; the uses to which alfalfa can be, and is, put, in all parts of the State where it has got a foothold, make this one of the most important grasses ever brought to the attention of farmers. The small farmer who has five acres in alfalfa, especially in the southern half of the State, has a secure supply of the most nutritious forage for all the animals he needs to keep. Cows pastured on alfalfa, or, what is better, "soiled" on it, yield abundance of the best milk, cream, and butter. Farm horses, if not too hard-worked, will keep fat and strong on alfalfa alone. Pigs are very fond of it, and do well on it; chickens like it, sheep fatten well on it. It is green all the year wherever frosts are not too severe—almost all over the State, that is to say; and, with frequent irrigation, an almost incredible quantity of the best hay can be cut from it—seven or eight cuttings in the year, of from a ton to a ton and a half per acre at each cutting. It yields, in fact, so abundantly that in the great valleys it is no longer very profitable to sell it as hay; and those large land-owners who some years ago thought to increase their great fortunes by putting thousands of acres in alfalfa, and selling hay at high prices, have quickly discovered that there is no money in it for them. But to the small farmer, and to the careful stock-raiser on a small or moderate scale, it is a very great boon.

I have seen, in some parts of the State, alfalfa by the thousand acres; but I doubt if it was profitable. But I have seen, on hundreds of small farms, five and ten acre patches, which were indispensable to the comfort and well-doing of their owners. Five acres of alfalfa, cut several times a year and judiciously fed out, and pastured at other times, will support— according to the general testimony of farmers with whom I have spoken of it—a span of horses, a cow or two, and yield besides some green food for pigs and fowls. In the San Joaquin Valley it is an established fact that alfalfa will support ten sheep to the acre the year round, and keep them in good condition; and with care it will, I believe, support twelve or thirteen head per acre.

For alfalfa water is indispensable. It requires irrigation; languishes, even when fairly rooted, unless it gets a frequent soaking—after every mowing is the rule—but makes a growth rapid and healthful beyond the belief of one who has not seen it, if it has proper treatment. Its roots strike deep, and it thrives best, therefore, in a somewhat loose soil, and repays careful and deep tillage as a preparation for the seed, which is very small. It will, I suspect, well repay frequent manuring, although this is not yet much practised here. Well put in, it has so far shown no signs of failure, even with the closest pasturing; and while it does not make what in the East would be called a firm sod, I have seen it quickly recover and densely cover the ground, after an application of water, where it had been fed down by sheep or horses until the ground seemed almost bare. Where farmers keep sheep and raise also wheat, it is customary for them to turn the sheep into the wheat stubble, to glean the field after harvest, which they do to their own advantage; and with this change of food, and the rest their absence gives to the alfalfa field, I have little doubt that in the southern half of the State even twelve sheep can be kept fat to the acre of alfalfa. It makes excellent hay, which, where it has been properly cured, and salted in stacking, cattle and sheep as well as horses eat voraciously, even when it is a year old.

It ought to be mown in the spring, when irrigation brings up in the field

POINT ARENA LIGHT-HOUSE.

great numbers of rank weeds, which animals will not eat, and which careless farmers too often allow to grow, to the detriment of their pastures. Cut at the proper time, when the summer heat begins, these weeds do not re-appear for that season, and the fields are beautifully green, lush, and smooth, giving a lovely aspect to a country-side in which this grass is used as it should be by the farmers. Irrigation, it should be remembered, brings a multitude of new weeds into the fields that are watered. The stream, drawn out of the mountains, not only gives life to the seeds of weeds already in the ground, but brings down myriads of others, which, stunted on the mountains, on the warmer plains and foot-hills would soon take possession if they were not met with the mower at the proper time.

Mr. Giddings, near Lemoor, in the "Mussel Slough country" of Tulare

County, one of the most intelligent farmers of that rich county, and himself one of the largest growers of alfalfa in his neighborhood, gave me the following details and figures, which are, I believe, trustworthy for the southern part of the State generally. North of Sacramento, where the winters are cooler and the rains more abundant, the management must be somewhat different; for three winter months this grass will not make a growth there, and at this time it ought not to be pastured. Mr. Giddings keeps sheep on three hundred acres of alfalfa, and raises no wheat, nor any other crop for market. To use his own words, he raises sheep for a living, and a few fine horses for his pleasure; and though, at the end of his sixth year from bare ground he has full-bearing orchards of apples, peaches, pears, plums, apricots, figs, nectarines, and a small vineyard of various grapes, he sells none of these products. With good land and a loose subsoil, he thinks five dollars per acre will sufficiently prepare the ground for the alfalfa seed. The method is to soak the soil with water, and as soon after as it is in proper condition to plough and cross-plough it, and harrow until it is well broken up and smooth, when the seed is sown, from ten to twelve pounds to the acre; or more, if the land is not very favorable. The seed varies much in price in different years, ranging from six to twenty-five cents per pound.

I should say that it would pay in most parts of the State to spend ten rather than five dollars per acre in preparing the ground for alfalfa; and as irrigation is necessary, it is required for this as for all other irrigated crops, to level the ground where the water will not cover it without. Levelling and grading I have described in the chapter on irrigation. They sometimes add seriously to the cost of land intended to be irrigated. In the "Mussel Slough country," on which Mr. Giddings's experience is based, a very great proportion of the land receives water, not by irrigation, but by what they call "seepage." The subsoil being very loose and porous, it is enough to run water ditches a quarter of a mile apart, through the land, and the water seeps or percolates, until all the intervening space is sufficiently moist for all crops, even for so thirsty a plant as alfalfa. But wherever water does not reach the subsoil one sees at once a barren spot.

Sown in January, it can be profitably cut in July, and will yield two cuttings the first year, besides a good deal of pasturage. To cut it for sale does not pay, except in the vicinity of cities or towns; but it pays handsomely to keep stock on; and the best way to do this is to cut it twice or thrice a year, and feed out on the ground where it is cut, so as to give the land the advantage of the cattle or sheep droppings. It needs no care when it is well set, but should be cut when it is about eight inches high. Sheep will pasture on it when it is that high, and they also eat the hay, and prosper on that.

Mr. Giddings pastures his sheep for nine months of the year in the alfalfa fields. During the other three months they have alfalfa hay thrown out to them, and get also some pasture when the winter is not too cold for this grass to grow. Keeping one thousand sheep on one hundred acres of alfalfa, the account, according to Mr. Giddings, would stand thus:

Land, at $30 per acre	$3000
Fencing	1500
One thousand sheep, at $2 50	2500
Putting land in alfalfa, at $7 per acre	700
	$7700
Interest on this, at ten per cent	$770
Expenses would be for shearing six cents a head	60
Attendance, two or three hours a week during three months, say	50
[The sheep need no herders.]	
	$880
Return: Spring shearing, $1 20 a head	$1200
Fall shearing, $1 a head	1000
Increase eighty per cent. = 800 sheep, at say $1 50 per head	1200
	$3400

This is counting wool at twenty cents a pound for spring, and eighteen cents for fall shearing, and the debit account omits dipping or other treatment for scab, and docking the lambs—but these, for one thousand head, would be but a small matter. The sheep, being in good condition and not crowded in corrals, suffer scarcely at all from scab. It appears that the net return, above interest and expenses, should be a good deal over $2000, and I have no doubt, in the hands of a careful farmer, would amount to $2500—a very handsome profit for very light labor, and with little or no risk.

When the agricultural land of California is enclosed for farms, sheep will be profitably kept on alfalfa as part of a varied agriculture; and a great advantage will be that they are always fat when thus kept, and that lambs, in the mild climate of California, can be produced in any month of the year fit for market. This is already done by some of the alfalfa growers, and at a handsome extra profit of course.

BOATING ON DONNER LAKE.

CHAPTER XIII.

IRRIGATION.

WATER can turn a desert into a paradise, and does it with marvellous rapidity. Seven years ago the " Mussel Slough country " was still a desert. Two years before that I drove over this region, and a sheep owner assured me that it afforded but a scanty subsistence for his sheep. But a number of farmers came and dug a ditch, led water in on their barren fields, and now it already looks like an old, settled farming country in the East, with shade-trees thirty and forty feet high along the roads, and apples, pears, plums, prunes, and vines in bearing. Where nine years ago ten acres did not fairly support one sheep, now ten sheep fatten on a single acre, and cannot keep down the alfalfa. It is a marvellous sight, this rapid growth and maturity of trees and all vegetation, under the stimulus of the sun, on land to which water is applied.

In the last ten years a great number of irrigating ditches and canals have been built in California; some of them of great size and volume, built by capitalists at the cost of hundreds of thousands of dollars; more of them of moderate compass, built by farmers co-operating for the benefit of their own lands. Some of the great ditches have proved unprofitable to their owners; but there is scarcely a farmer's ditch that has not been successful.

In the northern part of the State irrigation is not necessary, though it is useful in dry seasons, to which California is subject. South of Sacramento water is more necessary, and south of Stockton it is not safe to be without it. In average years the rainfall is sufficient to secure a fair crop of wheat or other cereals, but the dry years cause loss of these crops, except where water is applied; and to the small farmer, who does not intend to put a section of land (640 acres) in wheat on the chance of having rain enough to give him a crop, but who means to pursue a various and legitimate and safely profitable agriculture, water is indispensable. Fruit-trees and vines will not do without some water south of Sacramento.

Fortunately water is abundant. Most of the mountain streams from which irrigation water is drawn have very little water in the latter part of the summer, but that is happily the season when water is not used on the land. These streams have two annual periods of high-water—the first shortly after the autumn rains set in—that is to say, in December and January; the second in May, when the melting of the snows on the Sierras replenish them. Now, it is just when the streams are thus full that the farmers need the water; and this element is most abundant when it is most needed.

A careful survey of the water-supply has led capable engineers to the conclusion that there is abundance of it, for a proper use of it, for any population that will occupy the agricultural lands of California for a century to come. It is true that there are already disputes about water-rights, but these occur because some company of capitalists wishes to gain a monopoly of some source of supply, not because there is not abundance for all on any fair division. Enough water runs to waste every season now, in streams and ditches, in the southern counties, to irrigate millions of acres, where now tens of thousands are watered; and a close study of the map of any county in the so-called "dry" part of the State shows that whenever population comes to require water for land, it can get it in sufficient quantity. It will be a quarter of a century at least before reservoirs will come in use—though they have been talked of for some years; but whenever they are needed the foot-hills afford admirable natural depressions, surrounded by ranges of hills, and seemingly provided by Nature for the formation of reservoir lakes at a trifling cost. I have examined several such spots, with surprise at the ease with which building a comparatively narrow wall, a vast body of water can be stored, when, in the course of time, this shall become necessary.

Just now thousands of dry acres are getting water for the first time, and there is a great and extraordinary consumption, without the least sign of scarcity. It is a curious spectacle to see a part of the great plain soaked "for the first time since the Flood," as a farmer said to me. A furrow a foot or eighteen inches high is ploughed about a space of two or three acres, and the water is led into this square from the adjoining ditch. The earth drinks it in greedily; and by-and-by, after twenty-four or thirty-six hours, parts of the surface cave in, showing where gophers, badgers, and squirrels have built their extensive underground galleries for centuries past. The astonished animals rush to the surface, where blue cranes and hawks, hovering overhead already familiar with the operation, pick up the gophers and squirrels, while dogs and men kill the occasional badger. Nothing is droller than the impotent fury of the gopher, the most courageous little beast in the world, who, wrathful at his ejectment, rushes at the nearest living thing he sees with a savage little scream and vengeful eyes. The creature is no bigger than a rat, but I saw one make a gallant dash at a pair of horses one day, and at the owner's boots when he came up, not budging an inch until he was knocked on the head.

The soaking which large areas have thus received in the last three years has so filled the soil, that on many square miles the water in the wells has risen, in some cases from a depth of fifty feet, at which it originally lay, to within fifteen or twenty feet of the surface. Of course an immense quantity of water is required to produce so prodigious an effect over considerable areas; and the lower stratum being once filled, it is found that far less water is required for the subsequent irrigation of crops and orchards; only enough to maintain the waste which goes on from evaporation and capillary attraction. The universal experience is, that after the first thorough soaking a small quantity of water judiciously applied suffices for all the farmer's purposes, and that too much water is an injury to the trees and vines. Too many farmers, seeing the marvellous effect of irrigation on tree and all vegetable growths, imagine that they cannot have too much of so good a thing; and one sees too often vineyards and orchards, the property of thriftless men, where water has been set to do the whole work of the place, and ploughing and cultivating have been neglected, with the result that trees and vines are sickly and unfruitful. "To irrigate without ploughing and cultivating thoroughly afterward is ruinous," declared an experienced and successful orange and vine grower to me years ago; and it is the experience of every farmer I have met who uses water. "But to follow irrigation with thorough and careful culture is to insure prosperity and wealth," added this farmer; and this also has been confirmed to me everywhere in my recent journeys.

Where a number of farmers join to build a ditch or canal to put water on their lands, which is frequently done in this State, they usually incorporate themselves into a stock company, with a share of stock for every acre of land to be watered. They appoint from among themselves a board of directors, who cause surveys to be made, buy water rights if necessary, and then let the making of the main ditch or canal by contract.

DONNER LAKE, CRESTED PEAK, AND MOUNT LINCOLN.

When this is done each man leads the water upon his own land, and gates are made to shut it out or let it in at the boundaries. Such enterprises have been almost invariably successful, and in some cases where there was more water than the incorporators needed they have made money by selling the surplus to others below them. In not a few cases, where the incorporated farmers were too poor to pay out money except for surveys, they have turned in with their teams and made the canal themselves. After the completion of the work, there remains only a small annual charge for maintenance and repairs, and for the pay—very moderate—of the officers who regulate and guard the distribution of the water. Where men buy water of water companies, the charge is usually from $1 50 to $2 50 per acre for one application, or $5 per annum. Poor farmers who have no money to spare can generally get all the water they need in small places, by work on the annual repairs and maintenance of the canal near them.

In some parts of the State, as about San Bernardino and in parts of Los Angeles County, flowing artesian wells are used for the irrigation of alfalfa and orchard lands; and one flowing will sufficiently water twenty or thirty acres of land, and in some cases has been made to cover even more. Irrigation from canals is better, however, because this water brings down from the mountains a quantity of sediment which, deposited on the land, is a valuable manure. Where the subsoil is very loose and porous the canal or ditch water seeps into it, and moistens often a surprisingly broad tract adjacent, and this answers all the ends of irrigation, as the water thus seeping into the subsoil rises to the surface by capillary attraction, and keeps all beneath the surface sufficiently moist for the best plant-growth.

The question was often mooted formerly, whether general irrigation would not injuriously affect the health of localities. It seems from the best evidence attainable that it does not, but that, on the contrary, parts of Kern County, formerly very malarious, have become less subject to disease since the lower part of this county has been drained by numerous large irrigation canals.

Land to be irrigated must be so far level that the water, brought on from some point, will run over and, if necessary, cover it. For this purpose, where it is not originally level, it undergoes a process called levelling, or grading, in which, after it has received a thorough soaking, the plough and earth scoop are used to bring down slight elevations, and reduce the whole to a general level. This process, where it is done by contract as much of it is, costs from twelve to twenty-five or even thirty dollars per acre, and must be added to the first cost of the land. On large estates it is never thoroughly done, and the result of neglect is dry and unfruitful blotches in the fields. On small places it is usually done with care, and is a great convenience in all subsequent planting and cultivation. Land to be planted in orchards or alfalfa can well bear this charge, which comes but once. On the great plains large tracts of the land lie so flat by nature that levelling is needless. In the foot-hills irrigation itself is not so necessary as on the plains.

The actual processes of irrigation are various. In some parts orchards are irrigated by ploughing slight ridges midway between the rows of trees, each way. This leaves each tree the centre of a roomy square; and into each of these squares in turn the water is led, and allowed to soak until the ground is full, when it is drawn off to the next square. In other parts they prefer to plough several shallow furrows between the trees in one direction, and let the water run gently down these furrows.

The ridges or furrows are then levelled in the culture which follows irrigation, and the whole land lies smooth and fair; and, where the owner means to be successful, without a weed in a forty-acre field.

Alfalfa lands, where they do not get moisture by seepage, must be flooded, and this is done by what are called "checks"—which are slight ridges crossing each other, and from forty to eighty feet apart, as the lay of the land may require. The water is then let into the spaces between these checks, as in the other case, and allowed to run in until the ground is saturated. Vineyards are also irrigated by large checks, but the ridges are afterward ploughed down. The labor of thus checking the land is

CALIFORNIA LIVE-OAK.

not severe or costly, and is a part of the general and thorough culture which is indispensable, and which, I will add, makes a California orchard or vineyard one of the loveliest sights imaginable, to a farmer's eyes. The whole cost of irrigation of course varies, but may be estimated from the fact that, the cost of water excluded, the expense of thoroughly watering and cultivating an orange orchard or vineyard in the best manner is about twenty-five dollars per acre per annum. This, of course, does not include picking the fruit.

The most experienced farmers use the least water. Formerly it was thought necessary to drench orange groves at least six or seven times a year; now on the same land three, or at most four, irrigations are held sufficient. Formerly vineyards were watered several times in a season; now the best vineyardists irrigate once during the winter—which, they say, takes the place of a rainy season—and at most give one slight application of water in May.

Where wheat and other grain lands are watered, it is done before ploughing, and by large checks, or by furrows, as the case may demand, these ridges or depressions being ploughed out afterward. It is interesting to see how ingeniously the water is made to flow over and cover uneven ground, by irregular checks, and by leading it now from one side and now from the other of a field. The business is quickly learned, and the American already does it better than any one else.

THE BRIDAL-VEIL FALL.

CHAPTER XIV.

SETTLEMENT IN COLONIES.

CALIFORNIA was made by Providence for small farmers. Until very recently this was denied or doubted by Californians themselves, who protested—the more vehemently the earlier they had come into the State—that it was in the main only fit for great estates, on which capitalists, living in San Francisco, could raise cattle, sheep, and wheat, in a loose, wasteful way, by the help of Mexicans, Indians, and Chinese, with some Pike vagabond for a foreman.

Nevertheless, the farmers have steadily encroached on the large landholders; and while the passion for "big" estates has by no means died out, and men are still found rash enough to hold 20,000 acres in wheat, and plant 1000 acres in vineyards, prudent men, who are not dreamers, see that these great adventures in land are too hazardous; while the ugly fact that almost all the great estate owners are in debt, and in course of being swallowed up by their creditors, with only a "gambling chance" of saving themselves, shows more and more clearly that the small farmers —the forty and eighty acre men—are those with whom real and lasting prosperity will remain.

The adoption of the "no fence law," in 1873, was the turning-point in California's prosperity. Until then cattle and sheep were the rulers of the plains; and in the San Joaquin Valley and foot-hills—the "cow country," as it was significantly called—the owners of stock regarded it as an impertinence for a man to put a field into grain, and took particular pains to run their cattle through his wheat or barley, as the quickest way to ruin him and drive him out. Under the "no fence law" the owners of cattle and sheep are obliged to herd them, and are responsible for any damage their beasts do; and farmers are not obliged to fence their land. This last is, of course, an immense relief to settlers in a new country; and wherever in the State the farmers do not fence their fields, they secure themselves at least a year's start over those who do. In the numerous "colonies" fences are almost unknown, and one may ride or drive over miles of road, through pleasant fruit farms and grain and alfalfa fields, without seeing a fence. Hedges are, however, common in such localities, for these serve as wind-breaks, sheltering the young growth of fruit-trees.

The no fence law handed the State over to small farmers; but the area of tillable lands is so vast that the small farmer, in the true sense of the word, is still comparatively rare. In the great valleys, where wheat is the main crop, a man calls himself a small farmer if he has three hundred and twenty acres; it is only gradually that people are getting convinced, by the experience of others, that eighty acres is, in good localities, and with water, a little too much, and forty acres quite enough for a fair start in life. In my recent journey through the agricultural parts of the State, I have seen abundant reason for the statement which I here make with positiveness, that there are more prosperous and happily situated twenty acre farmers in California than there are of those who farm three hundred and twenty acres. The men of Anaheim, the first settlers, came without either capital or knowledge of grape or other culture— they were mostly San Francisco mechanics. They had a period of poverty, during which, however, they had abundance to eat, comfortable shelter, and not very hard work; so far as I could hear in my present visit to the place, all those who "stuck"—who were faithful to their vineyards, that is to say—are now comfortable, and many of them are wealthy. Now, these Anaheim men began with twenty acres and a town lot; and if any of them have more now, they have made it out of that original farm of twenty acres—with water. Near Stockton I noticed a number of very small farmers—men holding from fifteen to five acres—and all, without exception, had become fairly prosperous on even these petty holdings. Of one of them I was told this story: He is a German, having a wife but no children; in nine years he has, on five acres, cleared a mortgage off his place, and for the last two years has put over five hundred dollars a year in bank. He has four acres in grapes, which he sells at a neighboring winery; and he sells a few vegetables in the Stockton market. But he cultivates his vineyard carefully; and the man who buys his grapes told me that it yields from five to nine tons per acre. In the last ten years he has probably received twenty dollars a ton for these grapes—the product of his own labor, with a trifling expense for picking added. In the Central and Washington Colonies, in Fresno County, those who have held twenty acres long enough to have their vines and trees in bearing, and who have done justice to the soil, are safely prosperous. At Riverside, on what seemed to me ten years ago the most hopeless tract I saw in California devoted to small farms, a number of families have attained a degree of prosperity which is amazing even to Californians, to whom Riverside has become a synonyme for comfort and well-doing. Yet nine years ago, in my judgment, who then saw this tract set out with young orange-trees which had just been cut down to the ground with frost, and covered with shanties in which their owners shivered on a cold morning in spring, it was the least hopeful or encouraging enterprise on which my eyes had rested. Now, after only nine years, I find Riverside famous the State over for its oranges, its raisins, and lemons; and the poor settlers, who then looked out of the doors of their shanties upon frozen trees, are now living in comfortable houses, and have, report says, many of them comfortable bank accounts. And while they were waiting for results—waiting for their vines and trees to bear, and learning their business—though they had little money, they had always enough to eat, and sufficient shelter; and living in a "colony," or settlement of small places, had the advantage of social intercourse, schools, and the wholesome action of mind upon mind.

To this last, indeed, I attribute, in a large measure, the remarkable success which the plan of settling in "colonies" has brought to farmers in California. The farmer of six hundred and forty acres, or of a thousand, is necessarily a lonely being; he must "go to town" when he feels the need of society; and too often going to town means only going to a grogshop, and spending money which his family needs. The small farmers have neighbors near at hand; they easily, and, as far as I have seen, invariably, erect comfortable school-houses for their children; their wives have wholesome access to society; plans, experiments, new devices, are talked over; if one has a good thought, all the others get the benefit of it; and, finally, when vines and trees bear, the aggregate product of the settlement is so great that merchants are attracted, and the product of each is more readily sold and brings better prices than if he had lived solitarily on a larger holding.

Travelling through California in the fall of 1881, after an absence of nine years, I am amazed at the great changes I find wherever small farmers have come in, with their careful culture and intelligent planting. Of Riverside and Anaheim I have spoken; but in many other spots more recently settled than these what I saw formerly as an apparently irreclaimable wilderness now blossoms with roses and bursts with fatness. Orange, Passadina, Duarte, and other settlements in Los Angeles County, are little gardens; and very lovely gardens at that, with oranges, lemons, limes, raisins, almonds, prunes, apricots, coming into bearing, and yielding such profitable crops that, where the farmer is not prosperous, he has only his own idleness and neglect to blame. Fresno County, which eight or nine years ago was given over to cattle, and where a man put in a hundred acres of wheat at the peril of his life, and with an almost certainty that cattle would destroy it before it was half grown, is now dotted with colonies, where, after five or six years only of settlement, trees and vines are coming into bearing, and the former desert has become a prosperous and happy "country side." The "Mussel Slough country," in Tulare County, over which I rode in 1872, when a sheep-owner told me it was too barren even to run sheep on without risk, has in six years assumed the appearance of an old-settled and rich farming country in the East; Grangeville is as umbrageous as though its trees had been planted for half a century; and I found apple orchards, six years planted, laden with fruit, vineyards in full bearing, and sheep kept at the rate of ten to the acre on alfalfa, and unable to keep the grass down, where on my first visit I was told it was hazardous to run one sheep over a dozen acres.

Observe that all this remarkable change is due to small farmers. It is they who have discovered, year after year, what the land and the climate of California will produce. Mr. Blowers on forty acres perfected the raisin culture; in the Sacramento Valley small farmers showed the value of apricots and prunes, which, bearing in half the time required by oranges, are now thought to yield almost as handsomely as the orange.

Small farmers have introduced the very profitable dried-fruit business. In the "Mussel Slough country," small farmers have brought alfalfa to its greatest perfection — that greatest boon to the small farmer in this State, who finds that on four or five acres of this grass he can subsist all

MIRROR LAKE, YOSEMITE VALLEY.

the horses, cows, chickens, and sheep he needs for his household and his agriculture, and with no trouble except to prepare the ground well for it, and water it half a dozen times a year.

Observe, also, that this has been done by comparatively few men. The small farmers of the State are not yet a numerous body; their settlements or colonies are few in number, and thinly, very thinly, scattered over the State. There remains abundant room for thousands of such settlements on lands now untilled, or grown to wheat or barley, or run over by sheep. It is the belief of the shrewdest and most experienced men, and it is mine also, that the lands which can be most profitably and pleasantly taken in hand by small farmers are to a great extent as yet untouched by the plough. Usually they have sought the plains, because these were the most obvious places; but it is in the foot-hills of the

Sierra Nevada, both in the Sacramento and the San Joaquin valleys, that the pleasantest spots are found, as well as the safest climates for the more profitable fruits and vines. On the plains of Fresno and Tulare the progress of irrigation has produced sharp frosts, where frosts were before almost unknown, and the orange and lemon do not thrive except with such shelter as new settlers cannot give them. The vine is safe, and the raisin-grape does admirably there; but I noticed that the eucalyptus was injured, even when a tree thirty feet high, by last winter's frosts. But in the foot-hills no such severe frosts are experienced, and the few who have planted the orange in these hills have found them to grow safely. Moreover, for some years past it has become known that all the fruits—the peach, apple, plum, prune, cherry, apricot—bear better, and have a finer flavor and better keeping qualities, when planted in the foot-hills than when grown on the plains.

It is an advantage of the settlement of small farmers in colonies that they attract the best quality of labor. In all the colonies I have seen a part of the population consisted of men of small and sometimes of no means at all—men desirous to build themselves little homes, and who knew by experience that in such settlements their labor and that of their teams would be in constant demand. I have come upon many cases where an industrious German or Swede (oftener than an American, by-the-way) was paying for a twenty acre farm by the labor of himself and his span of horses; his wife and children taking care of a few acres of grapes or trees until they should come into bearing; and the vegetable garden, the chickens, and the pig and cow, which fed on an acre or two of alfalfa, supplying ample food for the family. Such men are certain to be comfortable and permanently prosperous after a few years; and in the mild winters of California they do not need to spend much money on houses or fuel, while animals need no shelter at all. The winter of this State is like the spring of the Eastern States or Northern Europe; and I have no doubt of the correctness of a statement made to me here, that what it costs a farmer in Iowa or Minnesota during three years to keep his house warm and his family clothed and cattle protected against the winter cold, would buy him a farm in California, and build him all the farm-buildings he would require here.

The settlement of "colonies" is likely within the next few years to have a considerable extension in California, as many of the great land-holders are tired of the cares and hazards of large estates, and are ready, if they only knew how, to subdivide their properties. In general it has been done in a somewhat crude way. Anaheim is the only "colony" settled by an organized body of men, who by their contributions bought the land, brought in the water, surveyed the tract, and laid it out upon a fixed plan for themselves. Usually a colony is a land speculation of a somewhat enlightened kind. A land-holder lays out a tract in twenty acre lots, marks out streets and roads, and offers the land for sale to whoever will buy, with a water right annexed by deed to every twenty acres. He appoints a resident manager, who, if he is a proper man, knows how to advise the new settlers as to planting and culture, and how to organize them into a society. In some instances regulations have been made concerning the sale of liquor at retail within the colony; but in general the chief object is to sell the land, and the settlers are left to their own devices. Even under this crude system prosperous and happy homes have grown up with surprising rapidity, and where the manager of such a land company has been an intelligent and careful man, he has the satisfaction of rapidly seeing the fruits of his labors, in the collection of a thrifty population, even where, as in some cases which I know of, the settlers were at first very poor. The Scandinavian Colony tract, so called, in Fresno County, has been "all sold out" in this way. It was a tract of less than three thousand acres, on which Mr. Henry, editor of the *Scandinavian Journal* at San Francisco, induced his countrymen to settle. He sold to them land, with water, at from fifteen to twenty dollars per acre, giving them considerable credit; and he told me that he was satisfied with the result, and, what to me was of greater interest, so were his settlers, who were originally for the most part very poor but hard-working people, most of whom paid for their lands by day labor on the lands adjoining the colony. The Central Colony, also in Fresno County, is a successful experiment of the same kind; still in its infancy, but with trees and vines well grown and, where the culture has been careful, bringing already prosperity and ease to the occupants. The Washington Colony, on a larger tract of land, is still younger, but promises well; and where the settlers were working-men their labor showed admirable results.

In all such adventures the land cost originally, and to the owner who laid out the colony, but a trifle—not over five dollars per acre: but he was at the cost of surveys, and of bringing water to it. This done, he retails his lands at from $25 to $50 per acre; water ditches, surveys, advertising, and management all making a total of expenditure which in some cases is quite large, and in some needlessly so. A large part of these expenses could be saved to the occupants by a more intelligent plan of settlement. A company of Eastern or European farmers and mechanics could easily buy, either on the plains or in the foot-hills, in the Sacramento or San Joaquin valleys, a sufficient tract to give them from forty to eighty acres of land each; and they could buy such tract at very low rates, often for not more than from four to seven dollars per acre. Such land should be chosen with care as to its quality, and with positive certainty that water can be led upon it; and for this the services of an expert engineer and surveyor are necessary. The digging of a water ditch can be done by contract. It is not a costly or difficult operation; and this done, the land is ready for the occupation of the colonists, and should not cost them up to that date more than twelve or fifteen dollars per acre. The example of the Anaheim settlement, of which I have spoken elsewhere, is useful for reference; and it is well to remember that the men who settled Anaheim were, without exception I believe, mechanics and laboring-men, who paid for their land and all the preliminary work on it out of the savings of their daily labor, not coming on the land until their vines were planted and about ready to bear a crop.

Settlements in colonies, as well as small farmers in general, have now a great advantage over those of Anaheim or Riverside. When these began the wine-grape and the orange were the chief reliance of such experiments. Since then the raisin-grape, the apricot, prune, plum, and a variety of other fruits, have been proved to be very profitable; and the use of alfalfa, as a cheap and constant forage plant, has become established.

In other chapters I have given details of the culture of the orange, lemon, lime, apricot, prune, raisin-grape, and of alfalfa and other products, as well as of wheat, and to these the reader interested in the question of farming in California is referred. But it may be asked, what should a man of narrow means do with a small tract of twenty or forty acres, by way of a fair and prudent beginning? This question I have put to a number of successful farmers, and some of their replies I will here set down:

I.—(This had reference, not to the member of a colony, but to a farmer settling for himself on land in a watered region.) A man should buy forty acres, for which, with access to water, he would pay from $20 to $40 per acre, paying a quarter down, and the rest after from five to seven years. He should have a team of horses, costing from $100 to $150; plough, harrow, etc., say $75; house, according to his ability, from $100 to $500. All the shelter needed by his stock he could build of poles, and thatched, at a cost of $10. He should put thirty acres in wheat, which in an average year would yield him clear money, after all expenses, $15 per acre, or $150; this because he needs cash in hand to pay for land and improvements. The ten remaining acres he should plant thus: half an acre in kitchen garden, which will supply his family all the year round. Two acres in vines for raisins, which will bear a crop the third year. Two acres in apricots, plums, prunes, peaches, and almonds if these last do well in his region. Finally, five acres in alfalfa, which will support all the cows and horses he needs, and a few sheep for mutton besides. A little Egyptian corn for his chickens will take up scarcely any space; and he has left, in this account, a sufficient place for his house and its comfortable surroundings. Wherever wheat is grown, there are people at harvest who go about with headers and threshers, and get in the crop for a reasonable price, so that the small farmer does not need tools for this. But the farmer of forty acres will have much time, after his wheat is in, in which, with his team, he can earn money by ploughing or other labor for other people; and in the harvesting season he can always make enough with his team in a harvest gang to cover the cost of getting in his own wheat, so that an industrious worker should make at least $20 per acre from his wheat.

Question.—Is there in such regions plenty of work for man and team?

Answer.—Always. Often he can earn his water for irrigating by working on the ditch; and good men can always get employment at from $1 50 to $2 without team, and $3 per day with a team of horses. A man coming into our country with a family and $1000 would have a fair start for a forty acre farm, and could take his pick of choice land. With half the money he could get on, but he would have to work hard for two or three years to get ahead.

II.—(This had reference to settlement in a colony, and B. is a settler in the Washington Colony, in Fresno County.) Twenty acres of land, with water guaranteed, would cost here, at $35 per acre, $700, of which a quarter, or $175, must be paid down, and the remainder can remain at interest for four or five years, and even longer if the buyer makes good improvements. To grade or level the land for irrigation would cost, if done by contract, from $15 to $25 per acre, but a farmer would do it himself at the cost of his own time and the service of his team. He should own a team of good horses, value $250; tools and implements, $100. He can put up a sufficient house for $250; his vines for raisin-grapes would cost him $15 per acre, and trees probably about the same—say $300 for planting his lot; and irrigation water will cost him here 62½ cents per acre, or $12 50 for his tract, for the year. His living he ought to get from his vegetable garden and the pigs and sheep he can keep on alfalfa. If he has no money left after planting his lot and building his house, he can always make what he needs by working with his team for others. In three years his vines will produce enough cash to pay all the expenses of that year, household and other, and leave something over; and the fourth year he may confidently expect to clear all that the land and the planting cost him, for in the fourth year he should get, and will get, from raisins or apricots, or even peaches, at least $150 per acre, clear of all expenses of that year.

Question.—Can a working-man, with a team, always get employment?

Answer.—Undoubtedly; there are never enough men ready to work on the land of others here. A man with a team can earn three dollars a day, every day in the year, if he wants to.

III.—(This was the agent of the Riverside Land Company.) You may say that I will guarantee sober and industrious working-men to let them have a tract of twenty acres, at the ruling price here now—from one to two hundred dollars per acre—without paying a cent down; and I will guarantee such a man work enough, if he has a team of horses, to pay for his land as rapidly as the payments we shall arrange become due. He shall only agree to build any kind of a house for himself on his place, and plant it with trees and vines, which we will show him how to do most cheaply and advantageously.

Question.—Then you like to see working-men with little or no money come into your colony?

Answer.—We need them all the time; and I will make good terms with all who are industrious and sober, as well as show them that they can have the best of chances here to make themselves comfortable and independent homesteads.

IV.—(This was a wheat farmer and land-owner in Tulare County; and the figures represent the cost and average profit of wheat on land having water.) He writes me:

"That you may learn something of our cost of production of wheat, I herewith submit a summary item of receipt and expenditure on a section of land in Township 18, South range, 21 East, in Tulare County:

Interest on $25 per acre, at 10 per cent	$2 50
Use of water and cost of irrigation	1 50
Ploughing	1 13
Seed (50 lbs. to the acre)	67
Bluestone (to prevent smut)	3
Sowing broadcast	10
Harrowing twice	35
Heading	1 87
Threshing	2 56
Board of threshing crew	33
Sacks, at 10 cents	1 47
Twine	4
Hauling	75
Per acre	$13 30

Yield, 1980 lbs. per acre, or 33 bushels per acre, average cost per ctl. 67 cents, realized $1 45 per ctl. $28 71
Its cost per acre 13 30
Net gain .... $15 41 per acre."

This year (1881) wheat brought a higher price than that given in this statement, and the profit of the farmer was, of course, greater. The statement is on the basis of a "section," or six hundred and forty acres of land—a square mile. I asked my informant if land must be purchased for such an operation. He replied, "No; there are many thousands of acres in Tulare County which can be rented for a price equivalent to one quarter of the crop, by men who have teams and tools to put in wheat; and land can be bought on credit also, by men who have capital enough to put in their crops." I asked, "Are there chances for men without any capital?" He replied, "Yes; there is always work enough for men who will work on the land among us. Farmers are ready to pay thirty dollars a month to men, and board them, and are glad to get steady, sober working-men; and in the harvest time the men in the harvest gangs get two dollars a day and food for two months and more."

I add here a brief account of the settlement of the Anaheim Colony—the earliest successful experiment in the State, and noteworthy because the colonists were not farmers, but for the most part city-bred mechanics and laborers; because they began so early that they had not the benefit of the large experience in varieties of grapes and trees which settlers or colonists at this time benefit by; because they did not select the best situation; and, finally, because they did, in spite of these serious disadvantages, achieve a notable success.

In 1857 several Germans proposed, in San Francisco, to some of their countrymen to purchase, by a general effort, a piece of land, lay it out into small individual farms, plant these with grapes for wine, and to do all this by one general head or manager, and in the cheapest and best manner possible.

NORTH DOME, YOSEMITE VALLEY.

After some discussion, fifty men joined to buy a tract of 1165 acres of land south-west of Los Angeles. They took care to get also a sufficient water-right for irrigation.

The land was selected and bought by the leader in the enterprise, Mr. Hansen of Los Angeles, a German, who had long lived in California, and who is a man of culture and ideas, and desired to see what could be done by co-operation in this direction. He became, subsequently, so much interested in the success of the plan he had formed, that he was the manager of the colony in all its preparatory stages; and as he is an engineer, and a capable, honest, and patient man, he was, I think, a very valuable person.

The Anaheim Company consisted, you must understand, of mechanics, in the main. There were several carpenters, a gunsmith, an engraver, three watch-makers, four blacksmiths, a brewer, a teacher, a shoemaker, a miller, several merchants, a book-binder, a poet (of course, as they were Germans), four or five musicians, a hatter, some teamsters, a hotel-keeper, and others: not a farmer among them all, pray notice.

Moreover—and this I say with a certain degree of hesitation—there is some reason to believe that the members of this company were not even eminently successful in their callings. They were not getting rich in San Francisco, where most of them lived. Several of them had money ahead, but most of them, I judge from what I hear, were men ready enough to better their fortunes, but to whom it would have been impossible to buy for cash a ready-made farm of even twenty acres.

Well, it was agreed to divide the 1165 acres into fifty twenty-acre lots, and fifty house lots in the village, leaving some lots for school-houses and other public buildings, fourteen in number.

The first contribution or payment toward the common stock bought the land. Thereupon Mr. Hansen was, very wisely, chosen resident manager, and the share-holders quietly went on with their pursuits in San Francisco, taking care only to pay up the calls on their stock as they became due.

It was the manager's duty, meantime, to go on with the improvement of the lots. This he did with hired labor—Indians and Californians.

He dug a main ditch about seven miles long, to lead the irrigating water over the whole area, with four hundred and fifty miles of subsidiary ditches, and twenty-five miles of feeders to these.

He planted on each twenty-acre lot eight acres in vines (8000 vines), and some fruit-trees.

He fenced each lot with willows, making five and a quarter miles of outside and thirty-five miles of inside fencing. These willows are now topped for fire-wood, and, as they grow rapidly, they give a very fresh and lovely green to the aspect of Anaheim. This done, he continued to cultivate, prune, and keep up the whole place.

At the end of three years, in 1860, all the assessments were paid: each stockholder had paid $1200, and a division of the lots was made. This was done by a kind of lottery. All the lots were viewed, and assessed at their relative value, from $1400 to $600, according to situation, etc.

When a lot was drawn, if it was valued at over $1200, the drawer paid the difference; if less, he received the difference. Thus, he who drew a

$1400 lot would pay $200; he who drew a $600 lot would receive $600 additional in cash.

When all were drawn there was a sale of the effects of the company—tools, horses, etc.; and, on balancing the books, it was found that a sum remained on hand which sufficed for a dividend of over one hundred dollars to each share-holder. I believe the actual cost of the lots was but $1080. For this each had twenty acres and a town lot 150 by 200 feet, with 8000 bearing grape-vines, and some fruit-trees.

Then most of the owners broke up at San Francisco and came down to take possession. Lumber for building was bought at wholesale; for so many families a school-house was quickly erected; shopkeepers flocked in and bought the town lots; a newspaper was begun; mechanics of different kinds were attracted to the colony; and the colonists themselves had at once about them all the conveniences for which, had they settled singly, they would have had to wait many years.

Now, it must be remembered that these colonists were not either farmers or gardeners by trade. Only one had ever made wine. They began as green hands; and some of them borrowed money to make their improvements, and had to pay heavy interest. They had to build their houses, make their gardens, and support their families. Here is briefly the result of the experiment:

1. There was a struggle for some years, but in this early time, everybody tells me, they all had abundance to eat, a good school for their children, music and pleasant social amusements, and they were their own masters. There is no winter here for the struggling poor man to dread or provide for.

2. Only one of the original settlers has moved away; and the sheriff has never issued an execution in Anaheim.

3. The property which cost $1080 is now worth from $5000 to $10,000; and I do not believe more than one in ten of the colonists would have been worth to-day, had they remained at their trades in San Francisco, any money at all.

4. There are no poor in Anaheim.

5. It is the general testimony that the making of wine and brandy has not caused drunkenness among the colonists. "When you see a drunken man in our town, it will be an Indian," said several people to me.

6. I have not a doubt that the moral standard of the people has been greatly improved. Their children are well trained; the men are masters of their own lives; they have achieved independence, and what to an

average New York mechanic would seem the ideal of a fortunate existence. The average *clear* income from their vineyards, which now contain mostly sixteen acres, is about $1000 per annum. Some few fall below this, but most of them, I was told, go above. They have besides this, of course, their gardens, which here yield vegetables all the year round; their chickens — in short, the greater part of their living. They live well; it is a land of plenty; and to me, who remembered how painful and unpleasant is the life of a mechanic or artisan in New York, it was a delight to see here men and women who had redeemed themselves by their own efforts from drudgery and slavery.

In repeating such an experiment, naturally, some improvements could be made. I think forty acres would be better than twenty; and this is the opinion of most of the Anaheim settlers. But forty acres are enough in this rich country. Then I should advise the planting of the raisin-grape, rather than vineyards for wine; or, if the settlers prefer to make wine, they should plant the finer kind of grapes only, and select their land with that view. Then they would plant nowadays not vines only, but also apricots, prunes, peaches, for canning or drying, and, if the situation were favorable, oranges, lemons, limes, in all their varieties. Thus they would secure many advantages unknown to the men of Anaheim when they began, and their profits would be both surer and greater.

VIEW FROM THE COULTERVILLE TRAIL.

CHAPTER XV.

HINTS TO SMALL FARMERS AND LABORERS.

I RECEIVE constantly letters from persons who, having read my account of the climate and agriculture of California, desire to remove thither, but want "some more detailed information." "What can I find to do out there?" is the commonest form such questions take. I propose in this chapter to give a somewhat particular reply to this question.

   1. In the first place, California offers, in my belief, the best opportunities for men willing to work on land that are to be found on this continent.

   2. It offers no opportunities at all for young men who want to follow sedentary or in-door employments. Clerks, no matter of what kind, book-keepers, writers of all kinds, California is full of. Idlers, city people, young men who want to dress nicely and do as little as possible—of all these it has much more than its share; and if any one who reads this

belongs to this rather large class, my urgent advice to him is to go anywhere except to California. He will starve there rather more quickly than in New York.

A friend of my own, some years ago, advertised in a San Francisco journal for ten active men, willing to work, to whom he promised thirty dollars a month and steady employment, without specifying the nature of the work. He told me that he was besieged the next day by an army of over two hundred men, all stout enough; but when he told them that he wished to employ them on farm work all but two departed with curses. They would not leave the city—and in the city they were mere idlers, "looking for a job."

To professional men, to clerks, to book-keepers, salesmen, to all who mean to or want to live by their wits, or by in-door labor, California offers less opportunity than almost any State in the Union. It is overrun with such people, and they are more helpless there, and more exposed to suffering, want, and degradation, than in any of the older States.

But to young men willing to work in the fields, ready to plough, to harvest, to care for horses, to do any and all kinds of farm work, it is a land of great promise. It does not matter much whether they know how to farm or not—it matters chiefly that they shall be willing to work, steady, industrious, ready to learn. Such men will not lack employment; they will find there, without difficulty, constant work, at good pay, with kind treatment; and when they have become accustomed to the life they will see more opportunities for advancing their fortunes there on the land, than anywhere else in this country.

Contrary to a too widely diffused belief, it is not a country in which men acquire wealth or competence suddenly or without hard work. What I like in California is, that with persistent labor on the land a man can there acquire means and a competence more quickly and more surely than elsewhere in this country. Labor is not needless there—on the contrary, the California farmer, to be successful, must maintain a cleaner and neater cultivation than we often see in the East. But, doing this, the rewards for his toil are much greater than anywhere in the East. And, moreover, the mild climate relieves him of a great deal of the drudgery and painful toil of the Eastern farmer.

Nowhere, either in America or Europe, have I seen such careful, thorough culture of the soil as in the orchards and vineyards of California. To the eye of a countryman no sight is lovelier than that of hundreds of acres all under the most perfect tilth—not a weed anywhere, not a furrow out of place, not a foot of soil neglected. This is what one sees in those parts of the State where men farm with brains, and where they know that such farming is sure to bring great results.

California is, as I have said in previous chapters, the land for small farmers. On twenty acres I have seen hundreds of men make a comfortable competence. Nowhere in the world is "a little land well tilled" so valuable and sufficient.

At the same time, in none of the States, except in Texas, is there to be found so large a body of fertile soil, cheap in price, easily subdued to the plough, and only waiting for the occupation of persistently industrious men.

Nowhere else does the soil favor so great a variety of products, most of them the world's staples, and now grown only in limited localities elsewhere. It is this which gives to the soil of the State its special and exceptional value, and makes agriculture there, far more than anywhere else in this country, a favored calling.

I have seen growing, with only common care, on one two-and-a-half acre town lot in Riverside, and all in bearing, oranges, apples, lemons, pears, figs, plums, apricots, almonds, quinces, grapes of a dozen varieties—but all what we here call hot-house grapes—prunes, pomegranates, peaches, English walnuts, and limes. The soil and the climate seemed as favorable to one as to the other of these fruits; the apples were as fair to view, as juicy and spirited, as though they had grown in New England, and they bore as well in six years as a New England or New York apple-tree at ten. It would be difficult to find outside of California such a collection in the same enclosure; but I have seen a dozen and could find a thousand localities there where, if the owners chose, they could make quite as varied a show.

Plant growth is more rapid and luxuriant in California than in any of our Eastern States. In Fresno County I saw last fall grape-vines, planted as rooted cuttings in the previous February, and receiving only irrigation and common field culture, which had made canes seven feet long and as thick as my middle finger, and in many cases contained bunches of grapes. At Riverside they showed me apricot-trees budded on almonds, one of which in sixteen months from the budding bore one hundred and seven pounds of ripe fruit. A farmer showed me two acres of raisin-grapes which were planted as "rooted cuttings" in the spring of 1877, and from which he made, in the fall of 1878, only eighteen months after planting, one hundred and forty boxes of raisins. In the following year his crop from these two acres, then less than three years planted, was five hundred and three boxes of raisins, which brought him over $600 clear money. In the fall of 1884 his net gain from the two acres was $727; and he and his son, a lad of sixteen, had done all the work on this vineyard, except five days of hired labor.

This man told me he had farmed in Iowa and Kansas before coming to California, and he had made more money from two acres of raisin-grapes than off one hundred and sixty acres of corn-land in Kansas or Iowa.

SECRET TOWN—TRESTLE FROM THE EAST, 1100 FEET LONG, 90 FEET HIGH.

From four year old raisin-grape vines another farmer showed me that he had netted last year $100 clear money per acre; and from six year old vines $200 per acre. In another case 136 budded lemon-trees bore, at five years, on a little over an acre of ground, $350 worth of fruit, sold on the tree, the buyer picking and packing them.

I could go on with such instances to the end of a long chapter; I give these only to show what the soil and climate do in California, with water and with careful, thorough culture. Without the last nothing will or ought to do well.

The healthfulness of almost all parts of California is another of its advantages to farmers and laborers on the soil. It is an admirable climate to work in. After the hottest days of summer follow always cool nights. Moreover the heat is dry, and, therefore, far more endurable. There are no such "muggy" and "sticky" days as we have in July and August, and this past fall I found days with the mercury at 100° in the San Joaquin Valley far less uncomfortable than a few weeks before I had felt other days in Ohio and Illinois, with the mercury marking 89° and 90°. An eminent German traveller and *savant*, Robert von Schlagintweit, wrote, some years ago, on this point, in a work entitled "Californien, Land und Leute"—California, its Land and People—"The climate of California, with all the varieties which it manifests in different parts of the State, is yet, undoubtedly, in a high degree healthful. He who comes to this State from the Eastern States of America wonders at the fresh complexion of the people; he is pleasantly surprised at their healthful color and the red blood in their cheeks, which he by no means com-

WINNOWING GOLD NEAR CHINESE CAMP.

monly meets in his home. It is not an over-statement that all California is exempt from a number of diseases which are burdensome and dangerous in other regions; so that one may here expose himself, without danger, in many ways which in other regions would entail serious consequences to the health. Only in low-lying lands, which, as some parts of the Sacramento and San Joaquin valleys, are subject to overflow, and of which the quantity is less now than formerly, is miasma found; but the spread of this is narrowly limited by the universal dryness of the atmosphere. A thoroughly or constantly sickly region is not to be found in all California.... Where else except in California would men venture to settle permanently on land where, for miles around, the beds of rivers and brooks are emptied by turning the streams, and the bottom, consisting of alluvial deposit, is turned over by the gold-seekers, or where they dig away the river banks, and so soak the earth with water that it steams during the warm days?"

"The climate of California," continues Mr. Von Schlagintweit, "on the whole, resembles that of Italy, but without the unpleasant peculiarities of the Italian climate, whose chief injurious effect is to indispose the people to labor of hand or brain. The *dolce far niente* of the Southern Italian is unknown in California. The peculiarities of the Californian climate, which distinguish it from that of the States east of the Rocky Mountains, are that the summers are cooler and the winters warmer, and that there is neither a frequent nor a sharp change from heat to cold, or the reverse. The air, too, is drier; there are fewer cloudy days, less thunder, and fewer storms than in the Eastern United States. To this must be added a circumstance most important and delightful to the inhabitants of California, that the nights are always cool and refreshing, even where, as in the low-lying valleys of the southern part of the State, the days are sometimes very hot. In some parts of the Sacramento and San Joaquin valleys the mercury rises at times to ninety-one degrees, and even, exceptionally, to one hundred degrees, in the shade; but the dryness of the atmosphere, which favors a quick dispersion of the perspiration, makes even this heat by far easier to bear than the same temperature in a damper climate."

The climate is everywhere most kindly to little children, which is perhaps one of its best tests. One cannot travel anywhere in California without noticing that the forms of the women who have lived some years here are more full and robust than with us; while the children are universally chubby, fat, and red-cheeked. I do not remember seeing anywhere in the State a single weakly or what the Yankees call "peaked" looking child. All animals also fatten easily here, and horses are very commonly so fleshy that they would be thought unfit to drive or ride in the East.

But "Is California a good place to go to for a young man without capital!" I am often asked. I answer unhesitatingly, Yes, if the young man is willing to work, and go to the land for his employment. There is, in all the agricultural parts of the State, a constant demand for "farm-hands." I should advise new-comers, laboring-men, to avoid the neighborhood of great estates. Where one owner raises wheat on ten or thirty thousand acres he needs men only during parts of the year, and turns them adrift for the remaining months, to recruit the too large force of idlers in San Francisco. But wherever small farmers have got a foothold, whether on "colony" tracts or elsewhere, there men who do not drink or gamble, and

VERNAL FALL, YOSEMITE VALLEY.

who are willing to work, can always get steady employment, the year round, at $30 to $35 per month and board; and a young man desirous to advance his fortunes can do so very well by taking such a place, and with his savings buy land as he sees opportunities offer. Since the adoption of the "no fence law" made small farming possible in the great valleys, there has been a constantly increasing demand for farm-laborers— a demand which the Chinese do not fill at all, because the kind of labor they furnish is useful mainly to the decreasing number of great capitalist farmers, and less useful to them than they originally believed.

The Chinaman still fills an important place in California country life, but the white man ousts him wherever he comes into competition with him for the best places; and this is going on so steadily that it is absurd to cry out against the Chinese nowadays. The small farmers, the one hundred and sixty acre and the forty acre men, have no use for Chinese. It is on the great ranchos and estates that they find employment. There is all over agricultural California at this time a large demand for honest and faithful working men and women. Women-servants receive from $15 to $25 per month, and, if only moderately capable, need never want employment.

For farmers of moderate means, say from $1000 to $3000, there are in all parts of the State profitable and pleasant locations in abundance; and, as my previous chapters show in some detail, a great variety of special crops offer themselves to such men, who need not undertake wheat culture, and, in my judgment, ought not to, because they can do better on small farms of twenty to forty acres with grapes or orchard fruits. I strongly advise new-comers with a small capital to content themselves with small farms; by good cultivation men make far more from twenty acres, rightly planted, than from a square mile of wheat.

Moreover, it cannot be too strongly stated that California is, for small farmers, still an open and almost unexplored land. The best lands are still cheap; the best locations are by no means all taken up; the most profitable cultures have but just fairly begun; and the farmer who settles himself out there in the next ten years has a better chance of success than those who settled ten years ago, because he has the experience gained in the past ten important years to go upon.

But—and this is my final word to all who may turn their faces toward California—it is no country for idlers or "clerks." It is a paradise for men who will work with their hands, and the better if they will also put brains into their work. One of the most successful orchardists I met last fall in the State was a Yale graduate, and not only that, but a member of "Skull and Bones," which places him among the *élite* of Yale. I saw nowhere more finely grown trees or better culture of the soil; and I met no one whose success was so declared and gratifying as his—achieved on twenty acres of land, carefully selected and faithfully tilled. In other parts of the State I met graduates of other colleges — men, also, not originally farmers, but who had found health and competence, and often wealth, in small farms, farmed with brains.

The settlement of Riverside is made up largely of men who were not originally farmers. In February, 1872, when I first saw this then new settlement, it seemed to me so deplorable a mistake, and so complete a failure, that I did not mention it in the first edition of my book. The newly planted orange-trees had been cut down to the ground by a sharp frost; the land seemed to me rough, and wanting in fertility; the shanties and cheap houses of the settlers had a poverty-stricken air. Now, in 1881, Riverside is the Californian's synonyme for success; the best raisins in the State are made there; their oranges and lemons bring the highest prices in the State; the houses are large and comfortable; and an unmistakable air of prosperity and fatness pervades the whole settlement, which

HYDRAULIC MINING AT FRENCH CORRAL.

is extending its bounds in every direction. There is no doubt that the early settlers, especially those who came, as many did, with entirely insufficient capital, had some lean years—years when they had little money to spend, and if they were in debt, a heavy burden of interest to bear. But those who stood by their places have been for some years out of debt and well-to-do; and many sold out their places only to buy and make new ones with the money they got, and are thus also comfortable and out of debt.

What Riverside was in 1872, that the Washington Colony, in Fresno

County, and a dozen others elsewhere, are now—they have the sure promise of success and prosperity for all who labor and wait.

What I wrote in 1874 the event has proved abundantly true—that any man settling himself on a piece of land in California, selected with common prudence, and who would till it carefully for ten years, would have a competence. And in that climate, the hardships of even actual poverty are not so great as to make manly men or womanly women repine.

OBSERVATION CAR.

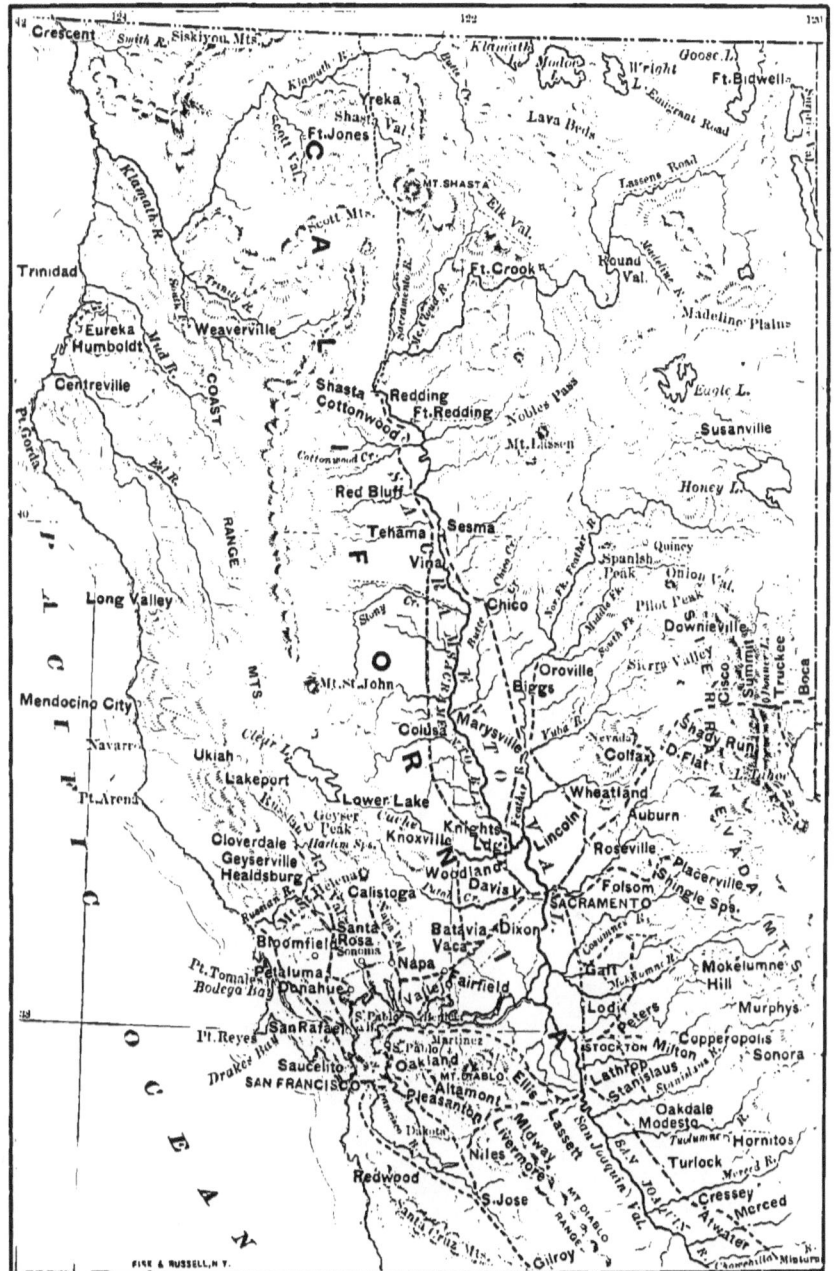

NORTHERN CALIFORNIA.

A QUARTZ MILL.

CHAPTER XVI.

A NIGHT AROUND A CAMP-FIRE.

"THAT a new place like Bakersfield should not have a church is not surprising," said I to the judge; "but you Havilah people ought to be ashamed that your town has neither church nor Sunday-school."

We were lying about the fire after supper, smoking our cigars, with that lazy contentment which follows a long day in the saddle. There were half a dozen of us—a Californian, who had lived in Arizona; an Englishman, who had lived in California; a Boston physician, whose name is not unknown to fame, and who has for some years played hermit in these mountains; our host, a sparkling combination of scholar, gentleman, and Indian fighter, the companion and friend of Kit Carson in other days, the surveyor of trans-continental wagon-roads, and the owner to-day of what seems to me the most magnificent estate, in a single hand, in America; and, lastly, the judge and myself.

"Californians may be a wicked set, as you Eastern people pretend," said the general, "but you must admit that they lose no time usually in building schools and churches."

He spoke the truth. Nothing has more constantly surprised me, in this thinly-populated Southern California, than to find everywhere churches and excellent school-houses. Even Bakersfield, which, when I first saw it, was but a town of yesterday, where the inhabitants had hardly a decent shelter over their heads, had a neat and roomy school-house—one of the most substantial buildings in the place.

"Therefore," said I, "it is the more abominable that you have no church at Havilah."

"Well," replied the judge, who was one of the leading citizens of that mining town, "I agree with you, and we did make an effort to get up a church, but somehow it did not succeed. My wife and I talked it over; she said she preferred an Episcopal Church, and I called a meeting of the most respectable men of the place to choose a vestry. They voted me into the chair, and I nominated Mr. Johnson for a vestryman. Mr. Johnson, who is a prominent citizen, declined to serve; he modestly said he thought himself not fit for the office; he liked an occasional game of draw-poker, he said; he was given to some other worldly amusements, like dancing, when there was a fiddler anywhere around; he couldn't resist a horse-race, and, unfortunately, all the horse-racing in Havilah took place on Sunday, which was sure to interfere with his duties as vestryman; and so he would rather not serve.

"I told him," continued the judge, "that men were not expected to be absolutely perfect in these days; that the chair itself was fond of an occasional little game of poker; and that the office of vestryman was, in the judgment of the chair, purely ministerial. But somehow he did not see it in that light; he is a modest man, and he wouldn't consent to serve. When he backed out everybody else did too, and so this effort of ours to get up a church fell through.

"I've always been sorry for it," added the judge, frankly, "for I think a church an excellent thing to have in a place."

Now, though we listeners may have smiled at the judge's story, he, I beg you to believe, was perfectly sincere in his regrets, and we could do no less than admit that he had "done his level best" in the matter.

"The fact is," said the Arizonian, "that Havilah is, like many mining towns, a rude place. I was going down the main street there one evening some years ago, when I got among a crowd of rough fellows, and I happened to say to Jack Thompson, whom I knew, that it seemed to be very quiet nowadays; I had not seen a man killed for a long time."

"'Haven't you? By the powers! come along with me,' said he, reaching around to the back of his trousers for his revolver, and grasping my arm. 'I'll show you how it's done; there's a whole billiard-room full of them up there!' and he waved his six-shooter over his head, and I believe if I hadn't quieted him down he'd have gone up and shot into the crowd. But that's some years ago, and they hung that scoundrel to a tree afterward, and that scared most of his kind away."

"The same fellow told me once," said the general, "of a little disappointment of his. He had a difficulty with a man, and no arms at hand except a shot-gun; so he 'went for him with the scatter-gun,' he said, 'and the contemptible weepon missed, and he just grazed him.'"

A FLUME.

"Your courts did not execute justice very vigorously in those days?" I suggested.

"Well, no," replied the judge, "they were too often like a judge they had in early days up in Tuolumne County. This judge had a quarrel with a lawyer, and the result was that he used regularly to charge the jury against any party whom this lawyer represented. At last Tom said one day in court, with some vexation, when he heard the judge begin to charge against him again, that he did not expect ever to get justice in that court. To which his honor replied promptly, and with contempt, that he would take d—d good care Tom should get no justice in that court."

"That fellow ought to have been a Tammany judge in New York," said some one, and turned the laugh handsomely against the East.

"It's astonishing," said the Englishman, "how rough and how ignorant men are who go about these mountains prospecting for gold. Some years ago, when the Temiscal tin mine was opened, and found to contain some valuable ores, there was great excitement around San Bernardino about tin. Dozens of people who knew nothing about indications of tin went out to prospect, and up in the Bainbridge District a fellow actually set up an assay shop, and made money for a month or two by pretended assays of the rock which credulous prospectors brought him. Of course he found tin in every kind of rock. It was discovered afterward that the scoundrel had stolen a pewter faucet, and made his assay buttons out of that. When that was used up he melted the solder from old tin cans for the same use."

"He ought to have been the man who told an English tourist, near San Bernardino, that up in the mountain there they had recently discovered a brass mine—'very rich ore, too,' he added, when he saw the Englishman open his eyes with amazement."

"We had such a fellow down in our country," said the Arizonian, "but he went off in disgust. He came into the hotel at Prescott one night, and at supper the landlord asked him if he'd have some teal.

"'What's teal?' says the fellow.

"'Why, a kind of duck,' says the landlord.

"'Had it wings?' says the fellow.

"'Certainly,' says the landlord.

"'And could it fly?' says the fellow.

"'Yes,' says the landlord.

"'Well,' says he, 'I don't want any, then; anything that had wings, and could fly, and didn't fly out of this accursed country, I don't want to have anything to do with.'"

"You've got some droll Pikes down there," said the general; "one of them met me once, and said he had travelled on the Gila with a certain person, a friend of mine.

"'You like that John Nugent?' he remarked; 'but he's a nasty little beast.'

"Now, Nugent was remarkable for his scrupulous neatness, and I said, 'I guess you must be mistaken; he always passed for a very clean man.'

"'*I* know him,' said the Pike, with a sneer of disgust; 'didn't I travel

A WATER-JAM OF LOGS, MENDOCINO COUNTY.

with him for three weeks down along the Gila River? And didn't I use to see him go down to the river every morning, with a dirty little tin cup, and a confounded nasty little brush he used to carry in his pocket, and scrub, and hawk, and spit, till it almost made me puke to see him? I tell you he's a nasty little beast.'"

"I believe there's not a hard story in this country that is not fathered either on Arizona or on the Pikes," said the Arizonian. "Yet our territory is one of the richest in the Union, as has been made known since Uncle Sam began to protect us against the Apaches; and as for the Pike, who is the hero of almost every California drollery, you all know that the Pike has many excellent qualities; he is hospitable, true to his friends, and though his ways may not be ours, and he is apt to think more of cattle than of other men, he is not, on the whole, a bad creature."

The Arizonian spoke truly; and, as I have in other parts of this book related some odd stories which are put upon the Pike, it is only right for me here to note this. The "Pike" is the "backwoodsman" of California; the name comes to him from the fact that among the early settlers of the State were many people from Pike County, in Missouri. "The Pike," said the Californian to me, "is only the South-western frontiersman; we got him because he was, as you know, always 'moving West;' and we keep him because here, no doubt to his own amazement and disgust, he butted up against the Pacific Ocean. He owns hundreds of cows, yet scarcely ever tastes milk; his wife still spins and weaves at home; and he and his family live here a thoroughly shiftless and happy life, and manfully resist civilization and its comforts."

"There is a fellow up in Colusa, whom they call Nick, a bar-keeper, who never tires of stories of the Pikes," remarked the judge. "He told me once that he had determined to keep the next fourth of July, having suffered one to pass over without any demonstrations. 'So this year,' said Nick, 'two or three of us took an old anvil down to the river, loaded it up, and began to blaze away. By-and-by I saw a lot of black objects bobbing up and down in the river away up stream. I thought they were ducks at first, but presently discovered them to be a lot of Pikes swimming the river, with their rifles held up out of the water. Soon they came along to us, and the headman, a gaunt six-footer in butternut, sung out to me, 'Stranger, whar's the war?'

"'I couldn't get their whiskey strong enough for them,' said Nick; 'so, after trying every way, I at last made a mixture of poison-oak and butternut. That fetched 'em. I called it the sheep-herders' delight; and it was a popular drink. The first Pike I tried it on yelled with delight; the next one took two drinks, and turned a double somerset in the road before the house. A peddler came along, and after taking several drinks of my sheep-herders' delight, he went off and stole his own pack, and hid it in the woods. When he came to himself he made a complaint of the theft; but I guessed how it was, and helped him to find the goods.

"'The poor old judge!' said the same fellow; 'he complained, on election evening, that he was quite worn out with signing checks all day.' I sincerely hope this was a libel on the court."

"Do you know how they carry on agriculture down in Arizona?" asked the judge, looking quizzically at the Arizonian. "There was a fellow who hired himself out as a farm-hand in Arizona, and the first day his master told him to cut some wood. So he asked for an axe, but the farmer said, 'No, we don't cut wood with an axe here;' and gave him a sledge-hammer to knock and break off the mesquit which they burn down there.

"The next day John was ordered to cut some hay, and was looking about for a scythe, when his master said, 'We don't cut hay with a scythe down here,' and gave him a hoe to chop down the woody stalks with which they swindle the horses there for hay.

FLUTTER-WHEEL, ON THE TUOLUMNE.

"The third morning the farmer called his man to come out and plant corn. John looked for a hoe, but his master said, 'We don't plant corn with a hoe out here,' and gave him a crowbar with which to punch holes in the ground, wherein to drop corn. They say John left the country in disgust."

"This country is quiet now," said the general; "but when I first came into it it contained some rough people. The head of the famous robber, Joaquin Murieta, and the hand of his lieutenant, Three-fingered Jack, were brought into my camp but a few hours after those two scoundrels were shot. Jack Powers and his gang used to herd their bands of stolen horses on my own rancho as they drove them through the country; and Jack once kindly came to tell me that he would kill the first man of his gang that took anything from me. Mason and Henry, the worst of all the road agents in this State, used to go through Kern County waylaying and robbing; and in those days a man had need to be careful, not only of his money, but of his life."

"They have a story here," said the doctor, "of a courageous woman in this county, who was alone in a stage which Mason and one of his gang stopped. The driver threw down the treasure-box when the two robbers stopped his horses, and Mason thereupon opened the stage door, and, leaning into the stage, ordered the woman to give up her money and rings, pointing a cocked pistol at her at the same time.

"The woman looked at him coolly, and said, 'Look here, don't you see that you're pointing that pistol directly at me, and that it's cocked? You seem to be a little nervous, for your hand trembles; I wish you'd point it away from me; it might go off and hurt me.'

"Mason was so much struck by the woman's coolness that, with an oath, he slammed the stage door, and told her to keep her valuables."

"She was lucky," said the Californian. "With these road agents you can't sometimes most generally tell how good-tempered they're going to be, or in how much of a hurry; and they are not always as polite as a fellow who, at San Luis Rey, in a written notice, 'begged to intimate to the public' that he was about to open a telegraph office."

Thus the stories went around until, one after another, we dropped to sleep under the clear sky of the mountain, with our feet to the fire and abundance of blankets over us.

To one who likes a free, out-door life I think nothing can be more delightful than the life of a farmer of sheep in the thinly settled mountainous parts of Southern California. The weather is almost always fine; neither heat nor cold ever goes to extremes; you ride everywhere across country, for there are no fences; game is abundant in the season; and to one who has been accustomed to the busy life of a great city like New York, the work of a sheep or cattle rancho seems to be mere play.

What we call at home a flock is in California called a band of sheep. These bands consist usually of from 1300 to 2000 sheep, and each band is in the charge of a shepherd.

Of course the sheep are scattered over many miles of territory, but each band has a limited range, defined somewhat by the vicinity of

TURNING A RIVER.

water, and it is customary in California to drive the animals every night into a corral, or enclosure, usually fenced with brush, and with a narrow entrance. This corral is near water, and the sheep drink at morning and evening. The shepherd sleeps near by in a hut, or, in the mountain parts, on a *tepestra*.

The corral is to keep the sheep together at night, and protect them in a measure from the attacks of wild beasts, which, curiously enough, are too cowardly to venture after dark over even a low fence.

The *tepestra* is to protect the shepherd himself against the attacks of grizzly bears, which are still abundant in the mountains, especially in the Coast Range. The *tepestra* is a platform about twelve feet high, built upon stout poles solidly set into the ground. Upon this platform the shepherd sleeps, in the mountains, at the entrance of the corral. The grizzly bear cannot climb a pole, though he can get up a tree large enough to give his claws a hold. It is, I believe, not infrequent for a grizzly to stand up at the side of a *tepestra* at night, and try to rouse out the shepherd. But all the men are armed with guns, which they carry day and night.

The grizzly does not usually attack sheep. The California lion, a strong but very cowardly beast, and not a lion at all, but a puma; the wild-cat, the fox, and the coyote, are the sheep's enemies.* The last-named is easily poisoned with meat which has strychnine powdered over it. The others are hunted when they become troublesome; and as the lion on the slightest alarm takes to a tree, and will run even from a small dog, it is not accounted a very troublesome beast.

Indians, Spaniards, Chinese, and some Scotchmen, serve as shepherds in California. The last are thought the best; and the Chinese make very faithful shepherds, if they are properly and carefully trained. They are apt to herd the sheep too closely together at first, from a nervous fear of losing one out of the band. Dogs I have found but little used on the sheep ranchos I have seen. They are not often thoroughly trained, and where they are neglected become a nuisance.

Of course the shepherds have to be supplied at stated intervals with food. They usually receive a week's rations at once, and cook for them-

---

* A sheep farmer in Santa Barbara County told me that one of his shepherds chased a "lion," in broad daylight, into an oak-tree, but unluckily had left his gun in his house, more than a mile distant. Determined that the beast should not escape, and knowing its cowardice, he took off his shirt, trousers, and hat, and placed these on sticks around the tree, in sight of the animal. Then, reduced to his shoes, he ran as fast as he could to the house, got his gun, and, on his return, actually found the lion still in the tree, and shot it.

selves. At the Tejon there are two supply stations; and every morning donkeys and mules were sent out with food to some distant shepherds.

The ration masters count the sheep when they deliver the rations, and thus all the bands are counted once a week, and if any sheep are missing they must be accounted for. The shepherd is allowed to kill a sheep once in so many days, but he must keep the pelt, which is valuable.

Above the ration masters are the mayor-domos. Each of these has charge of a certain number of bands; on a smaller estate there is usually but one mayor-domo. It is his duty to see that the shepherds are competent; that new pasturage is ready when a band has need for it; to see that the corrals are in good order; to provide extra hands at lambing-time; to examine the sheep, to keep out scab, which is almost the only disease they are subject to in this State; and to give out the rations for distribution.

On large estates, of which there are now a few left, there is, finally, a general superintendent, and a book-keeper and storekeeper; for here in the wilderness a supply of goods of various kinds must be kept up for the use of the people.

A blacksmith, teamsters, ploughmen, gardeners, and house-servants make up the complement of the Tejon's company.

COAST VIEW, NORTHERN CALIFORNIA.

CHAPTER XVII.

A CALIFORNIA CATTLE RANCHO.—A RODEO.—PECULIAR CUSTOMS OF THE SPANISH CALIFORNIANS.

FROM Anaheim a long but pleasant day's drive brought us, past San Juan Capistrano—which the readers of Dana's "Two Years Before the Mast" will remember as the place where he was let down the cliff some hundreds of feet to knock down a few raw-hides at the risk of his own skin—to the Santa Margarita rancho, then—ten years ago, in 1871 one of the great cattle ranchos of California, where I had been promised a *rodeo*.

The business of raising cattle was, as you know, for many long years almost the only pursuit of Californians. In Dana's time it was the great business of the province, and it remained for many years, in some parts of the State, the calling of a large number of people.

Cattle are not herded as sheep are; they roamed at will over large districts, and those of a dozen or twenty owners fed together on the pasture of all. Each man marked his own by a peculiar brand, burned into the left hip; and these marks, or "irons" (technically so called), were, like title-deeds of estates, recorded, and it was felony to obliterate them.

The "no fence" law of 1873 broke up the cattle-men, who had thereafter to herd stock on their own lands. Sheep replaced cattle in thinly-settled parts; but agriculture encroached rapidly even on sheep, the beneficent law really legitimatizing agriculture in the State. What I proceed to describe is, therefore, a reminiscence of past days.

Some there are, however, who regard regretfully the new era; they sigh for the free, open-air life of the plains—which in the climate of California

PIEDRAS BLANCAS LIGHT-HOUSE.

is so enjoyable—with the spice of adventure and danger which accompanied it. These are the "backwoodsmen" of California—only they had no backwoods, but broad plains, under their control; and they do not easily reconcile themselves to the presence of farmers, to the existence of wheat fields, or the growth of towns and increase of railroads. But their day is past. California is no longer merely a pastoral or a mining country. It is an agricultural State, with the advantage of producing nearly as much gold as in the past, and as many cattle as when, before 1873, the cattle-men controlled the great plains and turned up their noses at the farmers.

A RODEO.

The following copy of a public handbill will show the Eastern reader both the law and the practice which formerly obtained over a large part of the State, in regard to rodeos and branding cattle:

NOTICE!

OFFICE OF THE CLERK OF BOARD OF SUPERVISORS,
San Diego County, January 5th, 1872.

NOTICE is hereby given to all whom it may concern, that at a regular meeting of the Hon. Board of Supervisors, in and for the County of San Diego, State of California, on the Fifth day of January, 1871, it was, on motion,

ORDERED, That the following persons be, and the same were, duly appointed

JUDGES OF THE PLAINS,

to hold their office for the term of one year, and until their successors are appointed and qualified, to wit:

For the Coast Range.
Cave J. Couts,   F. P. Forster,   George Selwyn,   Juan Ortego,   James Kerren.

For Temecula Range.
Jose Valencia,   Juan Machado,   Jose A. Estudillo,   Francisco Estudillo.

For Agua Caliente Range.
Charles Ayers,   Joseph Sweikaffer,   J. Wolfskill,   J. Aguilar.

For Southern District.
J. W. Mulkins,   Boon Morris,   Francisco Ames,   William Cant,   R. K. Porter.

For Judges of the Plains at Large.
CHARLES THOMAS,   SYLVESTER MARRON,   JOSE ANTONIO SERRANO.

It was further Ordered, That the three Judges of the Plains at Large appointed as aforesaid meet together at San Louis Rey, in the County of San Diego, on the Second Monday in February, A.D. 1872, or earlier if they deem it necessary to do so, for consultation in all matters appertaining to their duties as Judges of the Plains, and to adopt such rules and regulations as may be authorized by law, governing and controlling their actions during their official term: and a portion of the duties of the said Judges at Large at their meeting as aforesaid shall be, and they are required to appoint the time and places at which all Rodeos for the County of San Diego aforesaid shall be commenced and continued.

And it was further Ordered, That for all services rendered by the Judges of the Plains, they and each of them shall have and receive from the parties required by law to pay the same, FIVE DOLLARS for each day for such services necessarily rendered by said Judges.

By order of the Board of Supervisors.

CHALMERS SCOTT, Clerk.

Sections 5, 6, and 7 of an Act concerning Judges of the Plains and defining their duties, passed April 25th, 1851, and the Amendment thereto:

ART. 2696, SEC. 5.—All persons travelling with cattle, sheep, hogs, horses, or mules, shall, in case said animals be not of their own mark and brand, be obliged to procure from the person or persons from whom they obtain such cattle, or from the justice of the peace residing nearest to the farm or place where they obtain the same, a certificate of the number and kind of such cattle, and the mark and brand which distinguished the same; and they shall allow such animals to be subject to the inspection of owners of lands through which they may pass, and upon arriving at any city, town, or village, shall present themselves to a judge of the plains, and state the number and kind of such animals; and it shall be the duty of the judge of the plains to examine the band or drove, and to accompany them out of the precinct of such city, town, or village.

SEC. 6.—That if the number and kind of animals do not agree with the report of the owner or person in charge, and with the certificates in his possession, the judge of the plains shall detain the band or drove, and take the owner or person in charge before the nearest magistrate for examination.

ART. 2697, SEC. 7.—The judge of the plains shall arrest and take before any magistrate any person who may be accused to him, or whom he has reasonable grounds to suspect of killing, hiding, or otherwise taking away cattle, horses, or other animals belonging to others, and shall execute any warrant delivered to him by any magistrate for larceny or other offence concerning said described property; he shall execute any warrant delivered to him by any justice of the peace, for the purposes herein named, and otherwise shall have and exercise the same powers as any sheriff, constable, or police officer, in the cases provided for by law.

When a horse was sold it was cross-branded—that is to say, the seller put his brand also on the shoulder, as a sign that his right is extinguished. Wherever a man saw an animal with his mark, he had a right to take it.

Every spring, in the cattle country, rodeos were held. *Rodeo* comes from *rodear*, the Spanish verb to gather or surround. A rodeo is, in fact, a collection of cattle or horses, made to enable the different owners to pick out their own, count them, and, if they wish, drive them off to their own pastures. It was held in the spring, because then the calves still follow the cows, and the great object of the gathering was to brand the calves.

Rodeos were held in the San Joaquin Valley at stated places and pre-ordained times; and one succeeded the other, going from south northward, until at last all the cattle had been seen, and all the calves branded. In San Diego County, where the Santa Margarita rancho lies, they began in the same way, far south near the Mexican border, and worked northward.

Sometimes 20,000 head of cattle were gathered on a plain, and the work of "parting out," as it was called, and branding, lasted for several days. A carefully defined set of laws regulated this work, and law-officers, called "Judges of the Plains," attended to settle disputes as to ownership, and regulate the procedure. These officers appointed the times and places of rodeos, and attended at each.

In the old times, I have been told, a rodeo was a formal and stately affair. It was held in turns upon the estates of different owners; and each entertained the assembled company. When I tell you that such a gathering commonly included from twelve to twenty proprietors, each attended by from six to fifteen vacqueros, and with six or eight horses for each person, you will see that there was a little army to keep.

But the old Californians were not only hospitable; they receive visitors with less inconvenience to themselves than any people I have ever known. I stayed one winter for some days, with my wife, at an old Spanish rancho, where the "house-keeping" was so quietly arranged that it seemed as though the house was empty; yet I learned, on inquiring, that from forty to forty-five persons, exclusive of servants, ate in the house every day while we were there.

Partly this is accounted for by the very simple habits of the people. They eat very moderately, and of few dishes, beef being, of course, the chief article of diet; and they sleep anywhere. Moreover, they drink only tea or coffee, and very little wine; they are very quiet and decorous in their manners, and they rise early.

In the old times, when the cattle had been gathered and all was ready,

SAW-MILL ON THE MENDOCINO COAST.

the mayor-domo—an important person on all these estates—came to the proprietor, with hat in hand, and formally announced that all was ready. Then the company, dressed in holiday attire, got to horse and rode out to the plain, and at the word the work began.

Then were seen some really magnificent feats of horsemanship; each vacquero vied with the other in this display; and as the day grew fresh horses were saddled, and no bull was so wild that he did not find his master.

The state and ceremony have gone out; but the skilful riding still remains in out-of-the-way spots, as well as the feats with the lasso, which are really like jugglery or witchcraft. I have a hundred times watched the fling of the riata, and yet have never in a single instance been able to detect the precise moment of the capture. But I am certain that a part of the trick is in the vacquero's intimate knowledge of the animal's motions; for I have seen a riata carelessly thrown down at a bull's heels, and, as the next instant he was fast, he must have stepped into the noose, and he who flung it must have known by experience what would be the animal's next motion.

At the Santa Margarita we attended a rodeo where the horsemen displayed in our honor some of their finest skill; and it was marvellous to see not only the certainty with which the lasso or riata is flung, and the admirable training of the horses, which co-operate with their riders and turn like a flash when a mad bull flies at his pursuer, but the jokes of the field. One of these is to single out a bull or cow, chase it out of the herd, dash after it at full speed, and lean out of the saddle until the rider catches the tail of the flying beast. This he winds quickly about his hand, and at the same time tucks it under his leg, holding it between the leg and the saddle. At the same instant the horse, feeling the tail on his flank, and perfect in his own part, increases his speed, and, both running in nearly parallel lines close together, if the horse's speed is greater than the bull's, the latter is flung heels over head. I saw this practical joke played a dozen times; it is one of the favorite diversions of the rodeo.

The rodeo grounds are usually permanent; and it was to me an odd fact that when the vacqueros went out to gather in the cattle from the hills and valleys for some miles on every side, they had only to begin driving, when all within sight turned at once to the big tree in the centre of the plain, where they were accustomed to be collected.

Half a dozen horsemen sufficed to keep a band of 2500 cattle in a compact mass for many hours. There were nearly a hundred horsemen on the plain; and as the coolest heads rode into the mass of cattle and singled out one by its mark, they turned its head out of the circle, drove it adroitly outside, and there two or three other horsemen stood ready to drive it to the knot to which it belonged, the calf frantically rushing after its mother, who turned again and again to see if it followed. This continued all day long.

At the house which entertained us more of the old Spanish Californian life remained than at any other I have visited. Spanish only was spoken in the family, and the old customs were kept up, not from any desire to be different from others, but because they were family habits. There is something very lovable and pleasant in these customs.

In the first place, the people are kindly and amiable; and though their pursuits might be thought to tend to loud and rough ways, and do so where our own people manage cattle, here all went on quietly and decorously, as though it was Sunday. The animals are handled firmly, but with great care and humanity. The work of the house proceeds with absolute noiselessness, and this though from thirty to fifty persons were fed at the house every day.

Spanish Californian houses, so far as I have seen their interiors, are always scrupulously clean; and, though their life seems to us strange, and does not comport with our ideas of comfort, it has the merit of fitting the climate and the pursuits of the people.

There remains in it, too, something which is too often lacking in our Eastern houses, a degree of trust and confidence and affection between master and servant, with not the least familiarity, however. I saw men —Indians—whose fathers had been in this same service, and of whom the proprietor told me that he would not hesitate to trust one of them with $50,000 to carry to the nearest town. The Spaniards know how to manage the Indians. Their self-restraint and courtesy have great effect. No vaquero addressed the master without either touching or taking off his hat. *Padrone* is the master's title. There was never any excited ordering about, and the work went on apparently of its own momentum.

In the evening the mayor-domo and the older vaqueros gathered on the long veranda. While a lady was singing in the parlor, where the family and visitors were gathered, I noticed three or four old men—evidently privileged characters—sitting quietly, listening, on a long bench in the hall. At meal-times, if the long dining-table was not full, two or three of these privileged characters quietly took the vacant places, far down — below the salt — ate and listened, or answered, if they were addressed. Meantime another long table was set, or had been set, under a piazza roof in the quadrangle which every Californian house encloses, and here others ate.

In the daytime this sheltered quadrangle accommodated three or four Indian women, who sat on the ground and did the family sewing.

People who rise early naturally go to bed betimes, and in the evening, after half a dozen cigaritos had been smoked, the company disappeared, to sleep soundly somewhere. As for me, I sat long and questioned our host's sons about the old times.

In the early days, it seems, the missions, which were then rich, made place and occasion for frequent festivities. To San Luis Rey, for instance, which lies near the Santa Margarita, came families from fifty miles around, with their retainers, for a fiesta. They remained a week or two, and the feast was partly religious, partly secular. The padres, rich in cattle, entertained all who came, and thus the country-side kept up acquaintance.

In those days, said my host, men used to travel from San Diego to Monterey, and never spent a cent of money. When night came you stopped at the nearest house. After supper you were shown your room. In the morning a clean shirt was at your bedside; and if you were known to the family, it was customary to place near the bed, on the table, also a sum of money, a hundred or two hundred dollars, from which the visitor, if he needed it, was expected to help himself. Lest my readers might think this incredible, I will add that General Vallejo has fully confirmed to me these and other particulars.

The next day a fresh horse was brought out and the traveller went his way. He usually carried with him a blanket, a hair rope to stake out his horse, and a riata, or lasso; and in a bag, tied to his saddle, a small supply of pinola. This is pop-corn, parched, and ground on a stone. It is mixed

SHIPPING LUMBER, MENDOCINO COUNTY.

with water and a little sugar, and a cupful of it makes, as I know by experience, a satisfying luncheon, if you have reason to expect a good dinner later in the day. To the abstemious Spaniard it sufficed, if occasion required, for breakfast, dinner, and supper; and when night came, if no house was near, he staked out his horse, often tying the rope to his own arm, that he might be awakened if the horse was startled by a wild beast; spread upon the ground the huge leather flaps which in those days loosely covered the saddle-tree, rolled himself in his blanket, and lay down to sleep upon the leather.

In San Diego County, I believe, it was a custom in the summer to guard against the approach of rattlesnakes by surrounding this couch with the horse-hair rope which is used to stake out a horse. This, made very ingeniously of the manes and tails of horses, is very rough, the ends of the hairs sticking out all over it, and these, it is said, the snake dislikes, as they probably irritate his skin; and feeling them, he turns aside.

Life on one of the old Spanish ranchos was, I am assured, not so simple as we have been accustomed to think. Various handicrafts had been introduced by the priests; and the Indians, who were the mechanics, were employed not only at the missions but by the more substantial rancheros. A gentleman at Los Angeles described to me the life on one of the great estates in that county "before the Americans came," and I may add that different persons, among them General Vallejo, have confirmed to me every detail.

They milked cows and made cheese; they dressed and tanned sheep and calf skins for clothing; they wove blankets; they made wine; they raised grain enough for their bread, and the Indian women ground this on stones; they preserved the hides of the cattle for the Boston ships; and at the San Fernando Mission, near Los Angeles, I saw the huge stone and cement tanks in which they melted down and kept the tallow, which also was sold to the Boston men.

"In those days," said my friend, "when I went out to see Don Tomas, he received me at the door; he showed me my room; and in a few minutes he came bearing in his own hands a basin of water for my use. But behind him came half a dozen servants, to show me that what he did was out of respect and welcome to me, and that servants were at hand to do it if he did not choose to trouble himself.

"This old man had sons and daughters, grown and married, living in his house. He always breakfasted alone, unless he specially invited his eldest son to eat with him. He arose somewhat later than the family, who had breakfasted before him—the men, I mean; for the women and children ate apart, and had a very merry time over their meals.

"When he had breakfasted he went out into his corridor or piazza. There stood his sons and his mayor-domo and his vacqueros, hat in hand. Then the horses, which had been saddled since daylight, were brought. The eldest son held his father's stirrup while he mounted; and when he was seated in the saddle the rest followed.

"Then he gave to each his orders for the day—to Martin the tannery, to Antonio the horses, to Tomas the cheese, or the calves; and when at last all this was received, always in silence, he gave the word, and out into the plain they rode as though shot from a bolt. The old man rode at the head; and as he galloped he called, in that low, soft voice which they almost all have, 'Pedro,' and Pedro drew up alongside; 'I do not want that mañada of horse on the hill yonder.' 'Si, Señor,' says Pedro, and gallops off. 'Antonio, these calves should not be here, they must be nearer the river;' and so on, always in a gallop, seeing everything with his practised eye, and issuing his commands as he rode.

"About four he returned to his dinner, which his sons ate with him. After dinner he sat in his corridor, made and smoked paper cigars, and contemplated himself.

"On Sundays and fast-days," said my friend, "the family rode to church, all on horseback—a graceful cavalcade, for the women rode finely, and the horses, which we Americans ignorantly despise, are yet the best saddle-horses in the world. (In this, by-the-way, every man who has ridden them will agree.)

"Then came the gold discovery, and the Americans, and the sudden and great wealth which spoiled all this simple life. Then they became too proud and too careless to milk, and so now you find no milk on the ranchos. They could buy clothing and all kinds of supplies, and so their useful and ingenious industries perished. They came to the towns dressed in absurd gold and silver lace, and with gold stirrups and gold-mounted saddles, and wasted their money in gambling-houses; and so their business was neglected. Finally, they thought it genteel to ride in carriages, and so they gave up the most graceful and healthful exercise which man or woman can have. I still remember my old friend Don Tomas standing here looking with silent disgust at his family climbing into a cumbrous coach, and then turning to me with the words, 'They are young and foolhardy, and may risk it, but for my part I am determined never to hazard my life in one of those things while I have strength to sit on a horse's back.'"

I do not doubt that it was a happy life they led—these old Californians. But it did not belong to the nineteenth century, and the railroad has left no vestige of it this side of the Mexican border.

But one thing I learned to admire among the old Californians which it is a pity we, their successors, have not copied from them; and that is the moderation of their lives. Their amiable and kindly temper, their abstemiousness, and temperance in eating and drinking, the readiness with which they submit to mere physical inconvenience, their kindness to dependents and servants, the skill with which they know how to manage these, and the politeness and ceremony which they carry into all parts of their lives, seemed to me very admirable indeed.

Going on from the Santa Margarita rancho to San Diego, I came there upon the story of a singular industry. The meat of the abelona shell, which is as much tougher than that of a Long Island quahaug as that is tougher than an old boot, is a delicacy among the Chinese. I do not know how they cook it — probably it is used to make one of the three thousand five hundred and ninety-two soups from which a red-buttoned mandarin takes his choice when he orders his dinner. The Chinese have discovered that this shell abounds on the coast of the Mexican province of Lower California, and particularly at Ceros Island. Two companies of Chinese have been engaged for several years, in those remote parts, in gathering the abelona meat; they work on shares, having a foreman or chief for each company, who attends to their business affairs. They remain on the island or the main-land, and a little schooner, owned by an old resident of San Diego who is also its master, carries down to these Chinese their supplies of provisions, and brings up the abelona meat in solid bales.

POINT REYES.

The Chinese cleave the shells from the rocks at low tide, and carry them up to the place where they are prepared. There the meat is cut from the shell and boiled; after boiling it is salted and dried; and when it is thus cured it is packed in bales, sent to San Diego, a ten days' voyage, in the little schooner, thence to San Francisco, and from there Chinese merchants ship it to their own country.

The schooner captain, a simple, honest old fellow, told me that he received an eighth of the gross product for carrying to the Chinese their supplies and bringing back their abelona meat; he was bound also to keep them in fire-wood, and to transport water for them, if they chanced to be working where no fresh water was near at hand. He told me that the Chinese were very honest, dealt with him always fairly, and "knew a

CENTRAL PACIFIC RAILROAD HOSPITAL.

heap more than some white folks." He remarked with wonder that they could all read and write. Will it surprise you if I tell you that most of the food which he carried down for this Chinese colony was imported from China? or that they live, as it seems to me, far better, and at any rate have a more varied bill of fare, than most of the ranch-men of California?

While we were in San Diego a party was preparing to go out into the mountains in search of a famous vein of silver, called the "Lost Lead," from the fact that it is known only by a tradition which reports that many years ago one Williams, who had befriended the Indians, was shown by them a deposit of silver of extraordinary richness in the mountains back of San Diego, and allowed to take from it as much as he wanted. The tradition adds that Williams went home with his silver, and lived in the East in comfort and independence until his death. He would not tell where he got the silver; and several parties have searched through the mountains since, with no success. They have found indications of silver, but no "Lost Lead." But when the young men have nothing better to do it seems the more adventurous of them get up a new expedition to look up this rich mine.

It may have been while a solitary adventurer was looking for this "Lost Lead" that he discovered an opal mine, from which he took for nearly a year stones, some it is said of fine color and considerable value. He too kept his secret—more difficult to keep than the mystery of the "Lost Lead." I was told that he had frequently been followed by curious or greedy persons, but without success; for he managed to baffle all watchers; and I could not help wondering whether the pleasure of eluding the trackers and setting at defiance public curiosity was not, perhaps, as pleasing to him as the gains of his discovery.

APPENDIX.

SOUTHERN CALIFORNIA FOR CONSUMPTIVES.

I SUBJOIN here a letter written ten years ago by a friend of my own, a consumptive, who, though since dead, experienced remarkable relief in Southern California, and, as he believed, added several years to his life by going there. The writer had spent several winters in Southern Europe and one at Aiken, and his letter, as well as the tables of temperature which he kindly added to it, compare the climates of these regions with that of Southern California; and his comparisons are too valuable to be omitted, though made some years ago. He wrote:

"Anaheim, Los Angeles Co., California, July 26, 1872.

" * * * You speak of the excessive heat. I do wish you and your family were in California; for a more perfect climate I cannot imagine.

"You ask me for some account of the climatic differences between some European and American winter resorts, and I send this to you, hoping that others may benefit by the information, as I might have done had I known what I now know; and I again repeat, with more confidence than ever, that had I come to California instead of going abroad, to-day I should be a well man.

"Mentone, Nice, and the Riviera generally, are the winter resorts recommended by the faculty, and they are, I believe, the best resorts in Europe; the others being far inferior.

"Meran, in the Tyrol, is too much shut in by mountains. The sun does not shine on the village until after it has been up for an hour, and a mountain to the south-west causes it to set upon the town at three o'clock in the winter. There is also a very cold draught that draws up through the pass.

"Vevey, Clarens, and Montreux, on the shores of Lake Geneva, are great resorts for French, German, English, and American invalids, and many go there because it is cheaper than elsewhere; but the climate only answers for the few. During the four months I was there we had no troublesome winds, but occasionally a *light* breeze.

"I found the climate of Clarens very soothing to the mucous bronchial membranes, but generally invalids did poorly there. It was by no means an unfavorable winter. Some seasons are better and others worse. It is an agreeable and, for those who are not ailing, a healthy place. There are good and comfortable hotels, at prices ranging from forty to sixty dollars per month, according to the accommodations. This account answers for Vevey, Clarens, and Montreux.

"Pau, in the Pyrenees, is much like Montreux in climate; perhaps two or three degrees warmer, and still more sedative, than the places I named on Lake Geneva. It is not stimulating, as on the Riviera, although more uniform and with less wind, and is very debilitating to many invalids. Some acquaintances of mine, who spent one winter in Mentone and did not like the winds, went to Pau the following winter, but returned to Mentone very much the worse for the experiment.

"The two winters I spent in Mentone, occasionally visiting the other towns on the Mediterranean for a change, led me to be most decidedly in favor of Mentone, as being the most sheltered and the best suited for invalids.

"San Remo I like next. Nice is a tiresome place for the sick, being too full of nonsense and fashion, with terrible winds and dust. The climate, however, is very stimulating and exciting, and cooler than at San Remo or Mentone. Oranges and lemons do not flourish there so well as at Mentone and San Remo.

"The first winter I spent in Mentone I did well, and but for the cold winds which blew I should have done very much better, for they gave me very many colds. I also suffered from the great difference between sunshine and shade. Even passing into the shade of a house was like going into a cellar, so great was the change. Many suffered from this cause much more than I did, for experience soon taught me to be extremely careful.

"From carelessness in guarding against cold winds, and the great difference between sunshine and shade, many left Mentone much worse than they would have been had they remained at home. The difference between sunshine and shade was generally thirty-five degrees. The temperature during the day in the winter season averaged fifty-five degrees, and the difference between wet and dry bulb thermometer five and a half degrees. Officers in health, and who stood the extreme heat of our Southern States during the rebellion, could not endure the sun in Mentone, but had to do as the rest of us did—use umbrellas. During the winter my sons, who often went on excursions to the mountains, always noted the direction of the wind, and we found that when we had the wind from a southerly direction it invariably blew on the mountains from the north; thus clearly showing that all the cold winds from the snowy Alps, after striking the ocean a few miles out, are reflected back on Mentone. The visitors as well as the natives suffer much from pleurisy, owing to these cold reflected winds, together with the great change between sunshine and shade. I always put on my overcoat when driving through the *old* town, as there was a chilling draught through those narrow, shaded streets. The new town is built on both sides of the old.

"The second winter I spent in Mentone did not agree with me as well as the first, as we had a *great deal* of wet and unpleasant weather. On one occasion I was confined to the house eight days on account of a storm; and the same winter (1868 and 1869) we had ice in the river at different times, lasting for several days at a time. The orange and lemon trees were much injured by the severe cold.

"A great objection to going abroad to spend the winter is the danger which the invalid encounters in the transition from land to sea, and *vice versa*. My experience among invalids is, that it very frequently results most disastrously, causing the patient to lose all that he had gained during a whole winter's sojourn abroad. When I went to Europe, and every time I returned, you know how I suffered from that cause; also when crossing the Channel from the Continent to England, as well as when I went South.

"Of all the Southern places of resort on the Atlantic side, Aiken and some parts of Florida are admitted to be the best. Florida has by far too damp a climate; it is not stimulating, but, on the contrary, very enervating. When I returned from Europe I did not know where to go. You *then* mentioned Florida; others spoke of Aiken; but my doctor did not like the latter place, telling me that he knew of many who had gone there, and that they did poorly. He advised me to inquire about Nassau, thinking that might be a good place. The following spring I met many who had spent the winter in Nassau, and they all told me that they would have been much better in almost any other climate than that, and farther said that it was very enervating; and, to their knowledge, no one who passed the winter there did well.

"You know what led me to turn my footsteps this way, and the result you know also. I shall enclose you an account of my meteorological observations for the winter of 1871–1872, and allow me to suggest that you publish them in full, for then an invalid could tell every day that would be fit for him to be out-of-doors.

"Southern California presents a most gloriously invigorating, tonic, and stimulating climate, very much superior to anything I know of; the air is so pure and so much drier than at Mentone or elsewhere; and although it has those properties, it has a most soothing influence on the mucous membrane, even more so than the climate of Florida, and without the enervating effect of that. It is quite as stimulating as Minnesota, without the intense cold of that climate.

"All the leading physicians of the world agree that a tonic, stimulating, dry climate is the best for the great majority of cases of suffering from pulmonary diseases or from a lowered vitality. The patient needs a climate in which he can spend most of the day out-of-doors. In Mentone, and in the towns on the Riviera, the doctors always advise the patients to be in the house one hour before sundown, the changes are so great; and not to go beyond prescribed limits, because the winds are too cold and the draughts severe. In California I have not been troubled in these respects; nor by the doctors, for I have not had to consult one since I have been in the State. As for going out, I have constantly been out evenings. During the past winter, out of one hundred and fourteen days I spent one hundred and six in the open air. This was in part of November, December, January, and February.

"Italy generally is a poor climate for the invalid, and the 'pure blue Italian skies' are not to be compared to ours; at least, with anything west of the Mississippi.

"I think the tables I send you clearly show that Mentone is by far the best climate in Europe for the invalid, and that California is far superior to Mentone. Such is the fact, and that is what I wish to convey. Yours truly,

"Francis S. Miles."

I add here tables of temperature, first for San Bernardino, during the winter months, November to March, both inclusive, sent me by the writer of the above letter, who was a skilled and careful observer. Also a table of temperature in Santa Barbara, by Mr. Tebbets, for the whole year 1881. San Bernardino gives the general inland temperature, and would cover Riverside, and even the San Gabriel mission. Santa Barbara lies on the ocean, but has its own climatic advantages.

AT SAN BERNARDINO, CALIFORNIA.

TAKEN 9 A.M., 12 M., AND 5 P.M., NOVEMBER.

WET BULB.	DRY BULB.	DIFFER- ENCE.	WIND.	REMARKS.	DATE.
53°	70°	17°	S. Light.	Bright sunshine.	November 8.
50	62°	12°	S.E. "	" "	" 9.
54°	67°	13°	S.E. Very light.	" "	" 10.
50°	54°	4°	E. " "	Clouds and rain from 1 P.M. till 8 P.M	" 11.
56°	68°	12°	S. Light.	Bright sunshine.	" 12.
50°	63°	13°	S.W. "	" "	" 13.
52°	64°	12°	S.W. "	" "	" 14.
50°	61°	11°	S. Very light.	" "	" 15.
52°	66°	14°	S. " "	" "	" 16.
50°	67°	17°	W. Light.	" "	" 17.
50°	64°	14°	W. "	" "	" 18.
57°	65°	8°	S.W. Very light.	" "	" 19.
55°	68°	13°	N. Strong.	" "	" 20.
51°	68°	17°	S. Light.	" "	" 21.
61°	78°	17°	N.E. Strong.	" "	" 22.
57°	70°	13°	S. Light.	" "	" 23.
55°	65°	10°	S. "	" "	" 24.
56°	60°	4°	S. "	Sunshine and clouds, and a light shower fifteen minutes, and rain at night.	25.
57°	61°	4°	W. Strong.	Cloudy and rain from 3 P.M.	" 26.
56°	60°	4°	W. Light.	Showery until 1 P.M., then sunshine.	" 27.
50°	56°	6°	W. Very light.	Sunshine and clouds.	" 28.
50°	56°	6°	N. Light.	" "	" 29.
46°	59°	13°	N. Strong.	Bright sunshine.	" 30.

251 11°. Difference between wet and dry bulb.
1469 = 64°. Average temperature.
Maximum, 79°; minimum, 45°.

DECEMBER.

48°	61°	13°	N. Very light.	Bright sunshine.	December 1.
48°	58°	10°	S. " "	" "	" 2.
52°	62°	10°	N.E. " "	" "	" 3.
52°	67°	15°	N. " "	" "	" 4.
55°	71°	16°	N.W. Light.	" "	" 5.
57	69	12°	S.W. Very light.	" "	" 6.
52°	67°	15°	N.W. Strong.	" "	" 7.
51°	67°	16°	S. Light.	" "	" 8.
51°	67°	16°	N.W. Light.	" "	" 9.
50°	64	14°	N.W. "	" "	" 10.
51°	68°	17°	N. Light.	" "	" 11.
49°	63°	14°	N.E. Very strong.	" "	" 12.
51°	67°	16°	N.E. Strong.	" "	" 13.
52°	63°	11°	N.E. Very light.	Sunshine and clouds.	" 14.
53°	67°	14°	S. Very light.	Bright sunshine.	" 15.
53°	58°	5	S. " "	Sunshine and clouds, and rain at night.	" 16.
53°	55°	2°	E. Light.	Sunshine and clouds.	" 17.
55	65	10°	S. Very light.	Bright sunshine.	" 18.
54	63°	9°	S. " "	" "	" 19.
55	66°	11°	S. " "	" "	" 20.
54°	56°	2°	S. Strong.	Rain all day.	" 21.
48°	52°	4°	E. Light.	Sunshine and clouds.	" 22.

APPENDIX. 203

DECEMBER—*Continued*.

WET BULB.	DRY BULB.	DIFFERENCE.	WIND.	REMARKS.	DATE.
49°	51°	2°	S. Light.	Rain until 3 P.M.	December 23.
54°	54°	0°	S. Very light.	Rain all day.	" 24.
55°	58°	3°	S. " "	Sunshine and clouds.	" 25.
54°	59°	4°	S. " "	" "	" 26.
52°	56°	4°	S. " "	" "	" 27.
56°	57°	1°	S. Strong.	Rain until 1 P.M.	" 28.
55°	57°	2°	S. Very light.	Cloudy all day.	" 29.
53°	56°	3°	S. " "	Sunshine and clouds.	" 30.
56°	57°	1°	N.E. " "	Rain all day.	" 31.

272 = 8⅘°. Difference between wet and dry bulb.
1899 = 61¼°. Average temperature.
Maximum, 83°; minimum, 43°.

JANUARY.

51°	53°	2°	S. Very light.	Cloudy most of the day.	January 1.
51°	55°	4°	W. " "	Bright sunshine.	" 2.
51°	56°	5°	S. " "	Sunshine and clouds.	" 3.
48°	57°	9°	N. Strong.	Bright sunshine.	" 4.
49°	56°	7°	N. Light.	" "	" 5.
52°	59°	7°	N.E. Light.	Sunshine and clouds.	" 6.
50°	56°	6°	S. Light.	" "	" 7.
49°	58°	7°	S. "	Cloudy all day.	" 8.
53°	56°	3°	N. Strong.	Rain all day.	" 9.
55°	59°	4°	N. Light.	Sunshine and clouds.	" 10.
53°	60°	7°	N. Strong.	Bright sunshine.	" 11.
54°	60°	6°	S.W. Light.	" "	" 12.
53°	61°	8°	S.W. "	" "	" 13.
58°	65°	7°	S.W. Very light.	" "	" 14.
58°	65°	7°	S.W. " "	" "	" 15.
58°	65°	7°	S.W. " "	" "	" 16.
54°	62°	8°	N. Strong.	" "	" 17.
56°	63°	7°	N. Light.	" "	" 18.
51°	60°	9°	N. Very strong.	" "	" 19.
54°	60°	6°	N. Strong.	" "	" 20.
52°	61°	9°	S.W. Light.	" "	" 21.
53°	60°	7°	S.W. "	Cloudy all day.	" 22.
51°	59°	8°	S.W. "	Sunshine and clouds.	" 23.
50°	60°	10°	N. Very strong.	" "	" 24.
49°	59°	10°	N.E. Strong.	Bright sunshine.	" 25.
44°	53°	9°	S. Light.	" "	" 26.
47°	55°	8°	S. "	" "	" 27.
49°	56°	7°	S. "	" "	" 28.
48°	55°	7°	S. "	" "	" 29.
49°	56°	7°	S.W. Light.	" "	" 30.
54°	56°	2°	S. Very light.	Cloudy all day.	" 31.

210 = 6½°. Difference between wet and dry bulb.
1798 58°. Average temperature.
Maximum, 67°; minimum, 38°.

FEBRUARY.

51°	54°	3°	S. Very light.	Sunshine and clouds.	February 1.
54°	60°	6°	S. " "	Cloudy all day.	" 2.
56°	60°	4°	S. " "	Bright sunshine.	" 3.
44°	57°	3°	S. " "	Sunshine and clouds.	" 4.
48°	61°	13°	N. Strong.	Bright sunshine.	" 5.
48°	63°	15°	N.E. Very light.	" "	" 6.
51°	63°	12°	N. Very light.	" "	" 7.
53°	64°	11°	W. " "	" "	" 8.
54°	59°	5°	S.W. Light.	Sunshine and clouds.	" 9.

APPENDIX.

FEBRUARY—Continued.

WET BULB.	DRY BULB.	DIFFERENCE.	WIND.		REMARKS.	DATE.	
55°	64°	9°	S.W.	Very light.	Bright sunshine.	February	10.
55°	61°	6°	S.W.	Light.	" "	"	11.
54°	61°	7°	S.W.	"	" "	"	12.
53°	66°	13°	N.E.	"	" "	"	13.
55°	67°	12°	S.W.	"	" "	"	14.
55°	67°	12°	S.W.	Very light.	" "	"	15.
57°	68°	11°	S.W.	Light.	" "	"	16.
60°	72°	12°	S.W.	Very light.	" "	"	17.
61°	74°	13°	S.W.	Light.	" "	"	18.
55°	67°	12°	N.	Strong.	" "	"	19.
56°	74°	18°	N.W.	Light.	" "	"	20.
56°	69°	13°	S.W.	"	" "	"	21.
51°	53°	2°	S.	"	Rain till 12 M., then sunshine and clouds.	"	22.
53°	60°	7°	S.W.	"	Bright sunshine.	"	23.
48°	51°	3°	S.W.	Strong.	Rain most of the day.	"	24.
48°	53°	5°	S.W.	Light.	Sunshine and clouds.	"	25.
50°	56°	6°	S.W.	"	Bright sunshine.	"	26.
51°	58°	7°	S.W.	"	Sunshine and clouds.	"	27.
46°	52°	6°	S.W.	"	" "	"	28.
48°	59°	11°	N.	Strong.	Bright sunshine.	"	29.

257 = 8½°. Difference between wet and dry bulb.
1793 = 62°. Average temperature.
Maximum, 81°; minimum, 47°.

MARCH.

54°	64°	10°	W.	Light.	Bright sunshine.	March	1.
55°	67°	12°	W.	Very light.	" "	"	2.
59°	71°	12°	E.	"	" "	"	3.
61°	71°	10°	W.	"	" "	"	4.
55°	59°	4°	W.	Light.	Sunshine and clouds.	"	5.
51°	56°	5°	S.W.	"	Bright sunshine.	"	6.
56°	63°	7°	W.	"	" "	"	7.
53°	62°	9°	W.	Strong.	" "	"	8.
54°	60°	6°	W.	"	" "	"	9.
61°	70°	9°	S.	Light.	" "	"	10.
59°	68°	9°	S.W.	Very light.	" "	"	11.
52°	60°	8°	S.W.	Light.	" "	"	12.
52°	62°	10°	N.	"	" "	"	13.
55°	62°	7°	S.	"	" "	"	14.
64°	69°	5°	S.W.	"	" "	"	15.
52°	59°	7°	S.W.	"	" "	"	16.
52°	64°	12°	W.	Very light.	" "	"	17.
63°	70°	7°	S.	Light.	" "	"	18.
55°	61°	6°	S.	"	" "	"	19.
54°	62°	8°	W.	Very light.	" "	"	20.
56°	63°	7°	S.W.	Light.	" "	"	21.
57°	62°	5°	S.E.	Strong.	" "	"	22.
56°	63°	7°	S.W.	"	Sunshine and clouds.	"	23.
55°	63°	8°	S.	Light.	Bright sunshine.	"	24.
57°	64°	7°	N.W.	Strong.	" "	"	25.
58°	66°	8°	W.	Light.	" "	"	26.
60°	68°	8°	W.	"	" "	"	27.
55°	62°	7°	W.	"	" "	"	28.
56°	62°	6°	S.W.	Very light.	" "	"	29.
57°	65°	8°	S.W.	Light.	" "	"	30.
57°	67°	10°	W.	Strong.	" "	"	31.

241 7¾°. Difference between wet and dry bulb.
1985 = 64°. Average temperature.
Maximum, 80°; minimum, 51°.

AT SANTA BARBARA, CALIFORNIA.

Latitude, 34° 26′; Longitude, 119° 43′. *Height above the Sea, 30 feet.*

FROM JANUARY 1, 1881, TO JANUARY 1, 1882.

BY G. P. TEBBETTS.

Months.	Obs.	1	2	3	4	5	6	7	8	9	10	11	12	13	14	15	16	17	18	19	20	21	22	23	24	25	26	27	28	29	30	31	Mean
January	a	45°	44°	45°	44°	43°	48°	40°	42°	44°	42°	42°	42°	44°	46°	54°	53°	48°	45°	43°	41°	47°	41°	43°	46°	47°	52°	45°	44	52°	55°	54°	46°
	b	58	63	62	60	58	62	58	58	60	57	57	57	58	58	57	56	59	59	58	56	62	66	60	59	57	60	60	58	58	58	60	59
	c	53	46	48	43	48	44	44	44	43	42	48	45	48	55	54	50	46	45	46	47	47	44	45	54	50	46	46	50	56	54	55	48
February	a	50	58	54	54	53	58	46	58	50	47	50	44	52	52	43	50	51	46	43	47	46	51	53	44	51	53	56	46	...	...	...	50
	b	63	68	60	65	67	63	63	69	61	60	59	60	60	61	59	59	59	60	62	67	69	78	77	60	61	68	63	68	...	...	...	64
	c	55	56	54	53	58	58	57	55	50	49	43	49	54	47	53	51	50	53	49	47	55	58	50	52	54	58	51	54	...	...	...	53
March	a	54	51	50	50	48	48	54	55	51	52	45	45	44	43	45	45	44	45	52	50	50	49	51	52	52	50	52	48	55	56	55	50
	b	61	68	68	60	64	61	62	53	58	59	59	64	56	52	55	54	58	62	66	70	60	66	57	59	61	59	68	68	70	70	58	62
	c	53	54	51	49	66	55	53	52	48	48	47	46	48	43	48	44	45	46	50	50	50	53	50	53	53	54	55	52	60	48	55	51
April	a	56	54	55	55	56	48	49	55	55	55	55	55	55	51	58	57	57	59	56	58	58	56	60	60	60	59	65	61	60	60	....	58
	b	61	61	61	58	64	63	64	61	65	62	63	63	68	73	60	65	60	60	67	65	60	69	68	74	76	74	77	68	68	65	....	65
	c	54	55	55	54	52	54	52	54	57	46	57	56	52	60	53	54	59	55	58	57	54	57	58	57	60	58	63	59	55	54	....	55
May	a	56	59	62	64	60	60	59	62	61	57	56	60	62	57	60	60	59	62	68	65	59	60	62	58	52	59	63	65	68	58	64	62
	b	64	60	69	73	68	67	71	68	72	65	68	70	72	67	63	67	68	72	74	72	67	67	67	65	62	68	67	68	73	69	71	70
	c	57	55	58	58	57	56	56	60	58	56	55	56	57	60	58	59	60	64	59	60	57	54	57	54	55	57	56	57	57	59	64	61
June	a	64	58	57	69	67	67	68	66	67	67	67	56	60	58	59	65	61	59	60	65	64	65	65	68	64	60	61	65	62	61	....	63
	b	70	67	66	73	78	69	74	70	78	69	70	72	70	68	68	75	68	65	70	73	70	73	74	70	69	71	68	67	69	69	....	70
	c	63	64	63	63	63	64	68	65	64	63	58	58	57	60	60	58	59	52	56	55	55	58	58	59	62	59	60	55	55	58	....	60
July	a	63	62	67	70	60	67	67	67	60	65	64	60	61	59	62	68	58	59	61	64	61	60	61	64	63	62	61	60	65	66	67	63
	b	72	77	87	76	73	78	81	73	73	71	71	68	65	61	72	75	68	69	71	73	69	71	75	74	73	71	71	73	75	76	76	72
	c	58	65	61	57	60	61	62	60	61	64	60	61	57	61	58	58	58	61	60	59	59	60	63	62	60	60	60	62	64	67	65	61
August	a	66	64	61	61	61	67	68	69	66	67	62	61	61	62	61	60	61	61	60	60	68	61	60	61	62	56	57	61	60	61	58	62
	b	75	72	71	74	78	81	84	83	79	73	74	68	71	66	70	67	73	73	71	74	72	71	72	71	74	74	73	75	70	70	68	74
	c	65	62	60	60	66	66	67	65	66	63	62	61	60	59	58	58	61	61	60	62	58	61	61	62	66	58	76	62	62	56	55	62
September	a	59	65	60	63	61	61	58	60	57	56	59	62	61	60	65	67	60	65	60	59	58	61	58	55	53	60	61	56	58	54	....	60
	b	73	71	72	70	70	70	71	74	73	70	75	76	77	80	79	80	71	71	72	70	70	68	68	75	72	68	68	70	72	76	....	72
	c	57	60	64	60	56	56	60	60	60	55	60	63	63	64	62	60	59	55	58	57	60	58	55	57	58	60	55	55	56	60	....	59
October	a	63	61	54	54	53	52	55	60	59	60	58	57	54	45	45	46	46	46	46	49	57	49	50	58	53	48	53	54	50	54	60	53
	b	72	68	70	73	70	72	68	68	65	65	63	66	65	68	65	65	70	73	68	64	66	68	64	68	55	61	64	63	69	70	71	67
	c	62	54	50	55	54	60	54	57	62	52	52	58	50	58	54	48	51	55	54	52	51	50	59	58	54	57	55	58	58	65	60	55
November	a	50	54	48	50	47	50	50	45	55	48	45	42	45	42	50	49	50	38	36	40	48	48	41	43	44	45	40	42	50	47	...	46
	b	70	73	71	72	64	60	68	68	65	68	65	68	67	65	60	60	58	58	60	67	70	67	70	73	72	72	64	60	60	59	....	65
	c	52	46	60	52	53	60	58	56	58	48	45	48	47	46	58	50	42	45	41	44	48	46	46	47	46	44	46	47	50	53	....	49
December	a	53	46	43	52	50	57	52	46	44	42	45	48	44	40	48	44	41	42	43	38	47	38	40	40	43	41	46	50	50	45	39	45
	b	57	57	58	62	63	63	65	61	61	58	57	58	59	65	56	61	61	61	64	65	63	61	60	50	60	58	57	58	71	72	65	61
	c	53	50	50	52	59	57	50	48	46	50	48	44	45	47	48	50	44	45	46	45	42	43	46	51	44	54	46	48	55	47	50	50

☞ The letters *a*, *b*, *c* denote the three daily observations: *a*, at 7 A.M.; *b*, at 12.00 P.M.; *c*, at 9 P.M.

APPENDIX.

HIGHEST, LOWEST, AND AVERAGE TEMPERATURE AT SANTA BARBARA, FOR EACH MONTH AND YEAR FROM JANUARY 1, 1871, TO JANUARY 1, 1882.

		January.	February.	March.	April.	May.	June.	July.	August.	Sept.	Oct.	Nov.	Dec.	Year.
HIGHEST.	1871	76°	68°	75°	83°	84°	79°	89°	90°	88°	103°	80°	72°	103°
	1872	72	73	74	75	94	100	82	96	84	88	81	79	100
	1873	76	67	76	80	78	80	86	82	83	82	82	68	86
	1874	70	69	70	78	78	82	86	88	83	72	78	69	88
	1875	73	77	76	86	95	80	84	90	83	72	78	69	95
	1876	73	71	74	86	80	84	84	83	83	85	81	75	86
	1877	83	70	76	73	75	102	87	82	86	77	82	74	102
	1878	67	69	69	77	77	76	80	84	94	84	76	76	94
	1879	68	79	80	83	92	97	80	85	86	90	77	73	97
	1880	70	63	68	69	82	73	75	77	85	81	77	70	85
	1881	66	78	70	76	74	78	87	84	89	73	73	72	87
LOWEST.	1871	40	40	46	46	52	56	58	60	54	48	40	40	40
	1872	38	42	46	47	50	57	60	60	58	49	51	41	38
	1873	42	40	48	46	54	58	58	61	56	50	46	40	40
	1874	38	41	44	50	53	56	58	58	57	52	48	43	38
	1875	40	44	44	41	50	54	58	59	57	52	48	43	40
	1876	40	41	46	47	53	56	59	60	56	55	46	43	40
	1877	42	46	46	50	52	58	61	58	58	46	49	40	40
	1878	38	41	46	46	52	57	58	57	56	52	41	37	37
	1879	38	39	46	50	52	54	58	59	55	50	42	38	38
	1880	33	36	39	46	51	52	53	54	51	41	36	41	33
	1881	40	43	43	46	52	55	57	55	53	45	36	39	36

RAINFALL.

Months.	1869-70.	1870-71.	1871-72.	1872-73.	1873-74.	1874-75.	1875-76.	1876-77.	1877-78.	1878-79.	1879-80.	1880-81.
July	....	....	....	....	....	....	....	....	....	....	.07	....
August	....	....	....	....	....	....	....	....	....	....	....	....
September	....	....	....	....	....	....	....	....	....	....	.11	....
October	.30	1.04	.09	....	....	1.91	....	....	....	.35	.41	.17
November	.65	.27	1.83	....	.27	1.30	6.53	....	1.41	....	1.93	.26
December	.57	1.41	6.56	4.34	5.26	....	.31	....	3.55	6.89	5.01	9.94
January	.25	.86	2.53	.58	4.54	14.84	7.56	3.04	7.87	4.83	1.42	3.02
February	5.87	2.92	1.81	5.48	3.17	.18	5.67	....	12.32	.72	11.50	.30
March	.83	.02	.18	.05	.78	.98	2.73	.61	2.68	.34	1 22	1.36
April	.99	2.02	1.80	....	.28	.10	.27	.39	3.31	1.80	6.25	.63
May	.74	.37	....	....	.14	....	....	.45	.29	.30	....	....
June	.07	....	.14	....	....	....	....	....	.05	.11	....	....
Total	10.27	8.91	14.91	10.45	14.44	18.71	23.07	4.49	31.51	15.34	27.95	15.68

Average for January, 54.32. Average for July, 67.40. Yearly average, 60.28. Difference between July and January, 13.08 degrees.
Average annual rainfall for 14 years, 16.91 inches.

NUMBER OF DAYS DURING WHICH THE TEMPERATURE FELL BELOW 43° OR ROSE ABOVE 83°.

	1873.	1874.	1875.	1876.	1877.	1878.	1879.	1880.	1881.
Below 43 degrees	7 days	9 days	4 days	17 days	15 days	24 days	13 days	48 days	29 days
Above 83 degrees	1 "	6 "	22 "	4 "	10 "	8 "	15 "	1 day.	2 "

Average below 43 degrees, 18½ days; above 83 degrees, 7½ days.

TABLE OF COMPARATIVE TEMPERATURES.

Location.	Winter.	Spring.	Summer.	Autumn.	Dif. bet. Sum. & Winter.
Funchal, Madeira	62.88	64.55	70.89	70.19	8.01
St. Michael, Azores	57.83	61.17	68.33	62.33	10.50
Santa Cruz, Canaries	64.65	68.87	76.68	74.17	12.03
Santa Barbara	54.29	59.45	67.71	63.11	13.42
Nassau, New Provid'e	70.67	77.67	86.00	80.33	15.33
San Diego, California	54.09	60.14	69.67	64.63	15.58
Cadiz	52.80	59.33	70.43	65.35	17.53
Lisbon	53.00	60.00	71.00	62.10	18.00
Malta	57.46	62.76	78.20	71.03	20.74
Algiers	55.00	66.00	77.00	69.00	22.00
St. Augustine, Fla.	58.25	68.69	80.36	71.80	22.11
Rome	48.90	57.65	72.16	63.96	23.26
Mentone	49.50	60.00	73.00	56.60	23.50
Nice	47.82	56.23	72.26	61.63	24.44
New Orleans	56.00	69.37	81.08	69.80	25.08
Cairo, Egypt	58.52	73.58	85.10	71.48	26.58
Jacksonville, Fla.	55.02	68.88	81.93	62.54	26.91
Pau	41.86	54.06	70.72	57.39	28.86
Florence	41.30	56.00	74.00	60.70	29.70
Aiken, South Carolina	43.82	61.32	77.36	61.95	31.54
Boston, Mass	28.08	45.61	68.68	51.01	40.60
New York	31.93	48.26	72.62	48.50	40.69
Denver, Colorado	27.66	46.33	71.66	47.16	44.00
St. Paul, Minnesota	15.00	41.29	68.03	44.98	52.91
Minneapolis, Minn	12.87	40.12	68.34	45.33	55.47

MONTHLY MEAN HUMIDITY, SATURATION BEING 100°.

January.	February.	March.	April.	May.	June.	July.	August.	September.	October.	November.	December.	Year.
71°	72	73°	67°	65°	69°	72	73	74°	70°	64°	64°°	62°½

Winter months, 69°.
Spring months, 68¼°.
Summer months, 71½°.
Autumn months, 69¼°.

MONTHLY MEAN TEMPERATURE OF SEA WATER.

January.	February.	March.	April.	May.	June.	July.	August.	September.	October.	November.	December.	Year.
60°	61	61°	61°	61°	62°	64°	65°	66°	63°	61°	62°	62°

THE ARLINGTON, - - Santa Barbara, Cal.

As there is but *one* Santa Barbara in the world, so there is but *one* Arlington in southern California. The rooms are large and elegantly furnished; corridors broad; grounds ample—4½ acres in extent—adorned with roses, shrubs, and palms.

Here the weary may rest; the sick be healed; the active roam over mountain, hill, and valley, or sail upon the ocean. Here is PEACE, HEALTH, COMFORT.

OJAI VALLEY HOUSE.

THE
Best Winter Resort in Southern California,

At NORDHOFF,

VENTURA COUNTY, CALIFORNIA.

— ••• —

The OJAI VALLEY HOUSE offers all the comforts of a country home. The table is supplied with the best the market and season afford, and with milk and cream from Jersey Alderney cows. Good saddle-horses and carriages, and lovely drives.

Parties will be met with conveyance at Santa Barbara, San Buenaventura, Newhall, or Santa Paula, on any day if desired.

For further particulars, address

FRANK P. BARROWS,
Nordhoff, Ventura County, Cal.

NORDHOFF, OJAI VALLEY.

OAK GLEN COTTAGES.

These Cottages contain from 2 to 8 Rooms each,

☞ ALL OF WHICH ARE SUNNY. ☜

They afford to families the advantages of a home without the cares of housekeeping; and, as they are clustered around the Central Boarding-House, where there are single rooms, society is at hand. Many of the rooms are 15 feet by 18 feet, and are supplied with open fireplaces.

The advantages of a climate beneficial to invalids, especially those suffering with pulmonary and asthmatic complaints, are probably more thoroughly combined in the Ojai than anywhere else.

Address

W. S. McKEE, Proprietor,

Nordhoff, Ventura County, California.

NEW COLORADO
AND
THE SANTA FE TRAIL.

By A. A. HAYES, Jr.

Illustrated. 8vo. Cloth, $2.50.

CHARLES NORDHOFF'S WORKS.

THE COMMUNISTIC SOCIETIES OF THE UNITED STATES: from Personal Visit and Observation: including Detailed Accounts of the Economists, Zoarites, Shakers; the Amana, Oneida, Bethel, Aurora, Icarian, and other Existing Societies: their Religious Creeds, Social Practices, Numbers, Industries, and Present Condition. By CHARLES NORDHOFF. Illustrated. 8vo, Cloth, $4 00.

Mr. Nordhoff has derived his materials from personal observation, having visited the principal communistic societies in the United States, and taken diligent note of the peculiar features of their religious creed and practices, their social and domestic customs, and their industrial and financial arrangements. * * * In pursuing his researches, Mr. Nordhoff was obliged to take extensive journeys, travelling from Maine to Kentucky and Oregon. With his exceptionally keen powers of perception, and his habits of practised observation, he could not engage in such an inquiry without amassing a fund of curious information, and with regard to facts which have never been fully disclosed to the comprehension of the public. In stating the results of his investigations, he writes with exemplary candor and impartiality, though not without the exercise of just and sound discrimination. He views the subject in its practical bearings, free from a cavilling and censorious spirit, and equally free from the poetical enthusiasm which would clothe a novel experiment with the coloring of romance.—*N. Y. Tribune.*

POLITICS FOR YOUNG AMERICANS. By CHARLES NORDHOFF. 16mo, Half Leather, 75 cents.

It would be difficult to find, indeed, a safer guide for a young man getting ready to "cast his first ballot."—*Nation*, N. Y.

A short and very clear account of the reason of governments, the things which government can and ought to do, and the things which it cannot do and ought not to attempt, and the principles which ought to prevail in its treatment, by legislation or administration, of the things which properly come within its province.

It is thus a treatise of political ethics and of political economy, and an excellent one.—*N. Y. World.*

It is a book that should be in the hand of every American boy and girl. This book of Mr. Nordhoff might be learned by heart. Each word has its value; each enumerated section has its pith. It is a complete system of political science, economical and other, as applied to our American system.—*N. Y. Herald.*

CAPE COD AND ALL ALONG SHORE: STORIES. By CHARLES NORDHOFF. 12mo, Cloth, $1 50; 4to, Paper, 15 cents.

Light, clever, well-written sketches.—*N. Y. Times.*

A lively and agreeable volume, full of humor and incident.—*Boston Transcript.*

STORIES OF THE ISLAND WORLD. By CHARLES NORDHOFF. Illustrated. 12mo, Cloth, $1 00.

A beautiful book, with pen-and-ink pictures of life in Madagascar, Java, Iceland, Ceylon, and New Zealand; admirably combining entertainment and instruction.—*Observer*, N. Y.

This charming little book, which will find its way to many hundreds of happy firesides, and gladden thousands of readers both old and young.—*Evangelist*, N. Y.

Published by HARPER & BROTHERS, New York.

☞ HARPER & BROTHERS *will send any of the above works by mail, postage prepaid, to any part of the United States, on receipt of the price.*

A CENTURY OF DISHONOR.

A SKETCH OF THE

UNITED STATES GOVERNMENT'S DEALINGS WITH SOME OF THE INDIAN TRIBES.

By H. H.,
AUTHOR OF "VERSES," "BITS OF TRAVEL," ETC.

WITH A PREFACE BY BISHOP WHIPPLE AND AN INTRODUCTION BY PRESIDENT SEELYE.

12mo, Cloth, $1 50.

"H. H." writes vigorously, is thoroughly in earnest, and desires to rouse the American people to a sense of the injustice and wrong done in their name to helpless, dependent creatures. * * * "A Century of Dishonor" deserves to be widely read, and in the poetess turned reformer the "children of the forest" have an able and eloquent advocate.—*Chicago Tribune.*

A number of striking cases of breach of faith, heartless banishment from homes confirmed to the Indians by solemn treaties, and wars wantonly provoked in order to make an excuse for dispossessing them of their lands, are grouped together, making a panorama of outrage and oppression which will arouse the humanitarian instincts of the nation to the point of demanding that justice shall be done toward our savage wards. * * * The book concludes with a valuable appendix, giving, among other matters, a clear account of the number, location, and condition of all the Indian tribes in the United States. * * * "H. H." succeeds in holding up to the public eye a series of startling pictures of Indian wrongs.—*N. Y. Tribune.*

Whoever has intelligence to understand and a heart to feel the grievances which the Indian tribes have suffered, as their lands have been steadily overrun and their possessions destroyed under the march of settlement, may find the narrative of seven prominent tribes impressively set forth in "A Century of Dishonor." Every page bears witness to the writer's research and industry, and to her heart-felt sentiments of humanity and justice. It is a volume of hard, sorrowful, undeniable facts in Indian sufferings. * * * She has collected from a variety of official, but not popularly accessible sources, a great body of information chiefly on the grievances of seven leading tribes; and she submits the tale, simply and lucidly narrated, to the common-sense judgment of the country.—*Christian Union, N. Y.*

The author of this book has brought to her task a ripe scholarship and a facile pen. More than this, she has evidently undertaken her work with an enthusiasm and a sympathy with the wronged which none but a tender-hearted and just woman can possess. * * * From its perusal the man who loves his country, and recognizes the universal brotherhood of mankind, will rise with genuine indignation, not unmingled with mortification and discomfort. * * * It is not possible that a perusal of this remarkable story of a nation's dishonor can fail to arouse the people of the United States to a sense of their own responsibility for the wicked dealings of their Government with the aborigines of our country.—*N. Y. Times.*

There was never so damning an arraignment of any civilized people. It is one terrible series of crimes and offences on the part of the United States Government against a weak and long-suffering race—a record of innumerable treaties made and broken; of lands foreibly seized; of horrible massacres and outrages such as South Sea Islanders could not parallel; of enforced starvation, sickness, and death. * * * We commend this volume to the reader. * * * In thus boldly championing the cause of the oppressed and in placing this record before the American people, the author deserves the hearty thanks of every one who has at heart the principles, we will not say of Christianity, but of humanity.—*Boston Traveller.*

A book with a distinct purpose to arouse, to excite, to move the public, and the purpose is one which deserves the heartiest sympathy. * * * She makes herself the advocate and champion of a cause and an oppressed people, and there can be no dispute about the main truth which "H. H." here seeks to impress upon the popular mind.—*N. Y. Evening Post.*

The Indian question has never had so thorough an exposition. * * * Simply as a book of reference concerning the treaties made and broken with various tribes, "A Century of Dishonor" is a most valuable book; and as a series of true stories it is painfully interesting.—*Philadelphia Bulletin.*

PUBLISHED BY HARPER & BROTHERS, NEW YORK.

☞ *Sent by mail, postage prepaid, to any part of the United States, on receipt of the price.*

www.ingramcontent.com/pod-product-compliance
Lightning Source LLC
Chambersburg PA
CBHW020913230426
43666CB00008B/1442